The Content of Our Character

The Content of

A New Vision of

Shelby

Our Character

Race in America

Steele

HarperPerennial

A Division of HarperCollins*Publishers*

"I'm Black, You're White, Who's Innocent" originally appeared in the June 1988 issue of *Harper's*.

"On Being Black and Middle Class" originally appeared in the January 1988 issue of *Commentary*.

"Affirmative Action: The Price of Preference" originally appeared in the May 13, 1990, issue of *The New York Times Magazine* under the title "A Negative Vote on Affirmative Action."

"The Re-Coloring of Campus Life" originally appeared in the February 1989 issue of *Harper's*.

"Being Black and Feeling Blue" originally appeared in the Fall 1989 issue of *The American Scholar*.

A hardcover edition of this book was published in 1990 by St. Martin's Press. It is here reprinted by arrangement with St. Martin's Press.

First HarperPerennial edition published 1991.

LIBRARY OF CONGRESS CATALOG CARD NUMBER 90-56430

ISBN 0-06-097415-X

91 92 93 94 95 MB 10 9 8 7 6 5 4 3 2 1

To Shelby, Sr.

Contents

Introduction

*"Of all that might be omitted in thinking,
the worst was to omit your own being."*

—SAUL BELLOW

On the afternoon of Martin Luther King's birthday in 1986,
I found myself half-listening to a radio interview with a local
black leader on "the state of black America." Long before
this afternoon I had begun to feel that public discussions of
the race issue had become virtually choreographed. Blacks
were expected to speak in tones of racial entitlement, to show
a modified black power assertiveness—not as strident as the
sixties black power rhetoric, but certainly not as ameliorative
as the integrationist tone of the civil rights era. Racism had
to be offered as the greatest barrier to black progress, and
blacks themselves had still to be seen primarily as racial
victims. Whites, on the other hand, had to show both concern
and a measure of befuddlement at how other whites could
still be racist. There also had to be in whites a clear deference
to the greater racial authority of blacks, whose color translated
into a certain racial expertise. If there was more than one
black, whites usually receded into the role of moderators while
the black "experts" argued. This is still the standard media
formula, the ideal public choreography of black and white.

It reflects, I think, the balance of power between the races that settled things down a bit after the turbulent sixties.

I cannot say that the two men I listened to that afternoon were lying to each other, or that much of what they said wasn't true. I can say, however, with much empathy, that they were boring, enough so that they received no more than a few calls on a call-in station whose switchboard is normally swamped. The source of their boringness, I believe, was that each man had left his full self at home and brought only the "received" part of himself to the studio. I can think of no issue that makes for a wider gap between the public and private selves than race. Publicly, we usually adhere to the received wisdom that gives us the most advantageous "racial face"; privately we are harassed by the uncensored thoughts and feelings that occur to us spontaneously. Race is an area in which Americans have been conditioned by a history of painful conflict into a rigid and unforgiving propriety. Each race has its politics and its party line that impose a certain totalitarianism over the maverick thoughts of the individual. Because of this we become a bit afraid of what we really think about race. And since we don't easily tolerate in others what we won't tolerate in ourselves, we tend to censor, name-call, and even purge those who let slip their real thoughts. Truth has a hard swim in waters where received wisdom so systematically dominates thought and intuition.

After this radio program, which was more a meeting of two postures than of two people, I picked up a pencil and began to write this book. I was tired of my own public/private racial split, the absence of my own being from what I said to people about race. The first paragraph I wrote remains unchanged as the first paragraph of the chapter titled Race-Holding. As the reader will see, that paragraph is probably filled with too much of myself. It was both scary and exhilarating to write because it portended a new looseness with the going racial propriety and a good deal of personal vulnerability. But I felt that if I could only stay with myself, I might get somewhere. I had no interest in writing autobiography or even in being autobiographical, only in following the road from the private self to the public reality. If there are inevitable distortions in this method, there are also distortions in every method. To posit anything is to be at risk. Though all the agonies of writing have been with me in abundance throughout the slow creation of this book, it has also been a joy to learn what I think.

In the writing, I have had both to remember and forget that I am black. The forgetting was to see the human universals within the memory of the racial specifics. One of the least noted facts in this era when racial, ethnic, and gender differences are often embraced as sacred is that being black in no way spares one from being human. Whatever I do or think as a black can never be more than a variant of what all people do and think. Some of my life experiences may be different from those of other races, but there is nothing different or special in the psychological processes that drive my mind. So in this book I have tried to search out the human universals that explain the racial specifics. I suppose this was a sort of technique, though I was not conscious of it as I worked. Only in hindsight can I see that it protected me from being overwhelmed by the compelling specifics—and the politics—of racial difference. Now I know that if there was a secret to the writing of this book, it was simply to start from the painfully obvious premise that all races are composed of human beings.

At this point I must acknowledge that I was helped immensely in this "technique" and the overall writing of this book by my wife, Rita Steele, who is a practicing clinical psychologist. Though her profession and the specialized knowledge it involves were helpful, these things do not explain her contribution. We both realize what an old professor of mine once said, that "ideas themselves come a dime a dozen." What one is after is the right *fit* of idea to reality. And reality must always have priority, accepting only those ideas that truly illuminate it. At any rate, this is the goal, and my wife's real contribution was her willingness to chew over endlessly with me the realities I struggled to explore. And lest "chewing" seem mundane, let me say that I know it to be everything. No page of this book is untouched by her effort, and many pages are the result of it. My children—son Eli and daughter Loni—not only endured a frequently distracted and ill-tempered father, but also shared with me their own thoughts.

I also wish to acknowledge Bill Thomas, my editor, whose encouragement, insightful criticism, and endless patience enabled me to make this a better book. No writer could ask for a more sensitive and understanding editor. I am also very grateful to Gerald Marzorati at *Harper's* magazine for his thoughtful editorial assistance and to the magazine itself for its belief in my work. Finally, I thank my agent, Carol Mann, for consistently sound advice. It has been encouraging to work with people who give their own being a place in their thoughts.

The Content of Our Character

1

I'm Black, You're White, Who's Innocent?

Race and Power in an Era of Blame

It is a warm, windless California evening, and the dying light that covers the redbrick patio is tinted pale orange by the day's smog. Eight of us, not close friends, sit in lawn chairs sipping chardonnay. A black engineer and I (we had never met before) integrate the group. A psychologist is also among us, and her presence encourages a surprising openness. But not until well after the lovely twilight dinner has been served, when the sky has turned to deep black and the drinks have long since changed to scotch, does the subject of race spring awkwardly upon us. Out of nowhere the engineer announces, with a coloring of accusation in his voice, that it bothers him to send his daughter to a school where she is one of only three black children. "I didn't realize my ambition to get ahead would pull me into a world where my daughter would lose touch with her blackness," he says.

Over the course of the evening we have talked about money, past and present addictions, child abuse, even politics. Intimacies have been revealed, fears named. But this subject, race, sinks us into one of those shaming silences where eye contact terrorizes. Our host looks for something in the bottom of his glass. Two women stare into the black sky as if to locate the Big Dipper and point it out to us. Finally, the psychologist seems to gather herself for a challenge, but it is too late. "Oh, I'm sure she'll be just fine," says our hostess, rising from her chair. When she excuses herself to get the coffee, the psychologist and two sky gazers offer to help.

With four of us now gone, I am surprised to see the engineer still silently holding his ground. There is a willfulness in his eyes, an inner pride. He knows he has said something awkward, but he is determined not to give a damn. His unwavering eyes intimidate even me. At last the host's head snaps erect. He has an idea. "The hell with coffee," he says. "How about some of the smoothest brandy you've ever tasted?" An idea made exciting by the escape it offers. Gratefully, we follow him back into the house, quickly drink his brandy, and say our good-byes.

An autopsy of this party might read: death induced by an abrupt and lethal injection of the American race issue. An accurate if superficial assessment. Since it has been my fate to live a rather integrated life, I have often witnessed sudden deaths like this. The threat of them, if not the reality, is a part of the texture of integration. In the late 1960s, when I was just out of college, I took a delinquent's delight in playing the engineer's role, and actually developed a small reputation for playing it well. Those were the days of flagellatory white guilt; it was such great fun to pinion some professor or housewife or, best of all, a large group of remorseful whites, with the knowledge of both their racism and their denial of it. The adolescent impulse to sneer at convention, to startle the middle-aged with doubt, could be indulged under the guise of racial indignation. And how could I lose? My victims—earnest liberals for the most part—could no more crawl out from under my accusations than Joseph K. in Kafka's *Trial* could escape the amorphous charges brought against him. At this odd moment in history the world was aligned to facilitate my immaturity.

About a year of this was enough: the guilt that follows most cheap thrills caught up to me, and I put myself in check. But the impulse to do it faded more slowly. It was one of those petty talents that is tied to vanity, and when there were ebbs in my self-esteem the impulse to use it would come alive again. In integrated situations I can still feel the faint itch. But then there are many youthful impulses that still itch, and now, just inside the door of midlife, this one is least precious to me.

In the literature classes I teach I often see how the presence of whites all but seduces some black students into provocation. When we come to a novel by a black writer, say Toni Morrison, the white students can easily discuss the human motivations of the black characters. But, inevitably, a black student, as if by reflex, will begin to set in relief the various racial problems that are the background of these characters' lives. This student's tone will carry a reprimand: the class is afraid to confront the reality of racism. Classes cannot be allowed to die like dinner parties, however. My latest strategy is to thank that student for his or her moral vigilance and then appoint the young man or woman as the class's official racism monitor. But even if I get a laugh—I usually do, but sometimes the student is particularly indignant, and it gets uncomfortable—the strategy never quite works. Our racial division is suddenly drawn in neon. Overcaution spreads like spilled paint. And, in fact, the black student who started it all does become a kind of monitor. The very presence of this student imposes a new accountability on the class.

I think those who provoke this sort of awkwardness are operating out of a black identity that obliges them to badger white people about race almost on principle. Content hardly matters. (For example, it made little sense for the engineer to expect white people to anguish terribly much over his decision to send his daughter to school with *white* children.) Race indeed remains a source of white shame; the goal of these provocations is to put whites, no matter how indirectly, in touch with this collective guilt. In other words, these provocations I speak of are *power* moves, little shows of power that try to freeze the "enemy" in self-consciousness. They gratify and inflate the provocateur. They are the underdog's bite. And whites, far more secure in their power, respond with a self-contained and tolerant silence that is itself a show of power. What greater power than that of nonresponse, the power to let a small enemy sizzle in his own juices, to even feel a little sad at his frustration just as one is also complimented by it. Black anger always, in a way, flatters white power. In America, to know that one is not black is to feel an extra grace, a little boost of impunity.

I think the real trouble between the races in America is that the races are not just races but competing power groups—a fact that is easily minimized, perhaps because it is so obvious. What is not so obvious is that this is true quite apart from the issue of class. Even the well-situated middle-class (or wealthy) black is never completely immune to that peculiar contest of power that his skin color subjects him to.

Race is a separate reality in American society, an entity that carries its own potential for power, a mark of fate that class can soften considerably but not eradicate.

The distinction of race has always been used in American life to sanction each race's pursuit of power in relation to the other. The allure of race as a human delineation is the very shallowness of the delineation it makes. Onto this shallowness—mere skin and hair—men can project a false depth, a system of dismal attributions, a series of malevolent or ignoble stereotypes that skin and hair lack the substance to contradict. These dark projections then rationalize the pursuit of power. Your difference from me makes you bad, and your badness justifies, even demands, my pursuit of power over you—the oldest formula for aggression known to man. Whenever much importance is given to race, power is the primary motive.

But the human animal almost never pursues power without first convincing himself that he is *entitled* to it. And this feeling of entitlement has its own precondition: to be entitled one must first believe in one's innocence, at least in the area where one wishes to be entitled. By innocence I mean a feeling of essential goodness in relation to others and, therefore, superiority to others. Our innocence always inflates us and deflates those we seek power over. Once inflated we are entitled; we are in fact licensed to go after the power our innocence tells us we deserve. In this sense, *innocence is power*. Of course, innocence need not be genuine or real in any objective sense, as the Nazis demonstrated not long ago. Its only test is whether or not we can convince ourselves of it.

I think the racial struggle in America has always been primarily a struggle for innocence. White racism from the beginning has been a claim of white innocence and therefore of white entitlement to subjugate blacks. And in the sixties, as went innocence so went power. Blacks used the innocence that grew out of their long subjugation to seize more power, while whites lost some of their innocence and so lost a degree of power over blacks. Both races instinctively understand that to lose innocence is to lose power (in relation to each other). To be innocent someone else must be guilty, a natural law that leads the races to forge their innocence on each other's backs. The inferiority of the black always makes the white man superior; the evil might of whites makes blacks good. This pattern means that both races have a hidden investment in racism and racial disharmony despite their good intentions to the contrary. Power defines their relations, and power requires innocence, which, in turn, requires racism and racial division.

I believe it was his hidden investment that the engineer was protecting when he made his remark—the white "evil" he saw in a white school "depriving" his daughter of her black heritage confirmed his innocence. Only the logic of power explained his emphasis—he bent reality to show that he was once again a victim of the white world and, as a victim, innocent. His determined eyes insisted on this. And the whites, in their silence, no doubt protected their innocence by seeing him as an ungracious troublemaker, his bad behavior underscoring their goodness. What none of us saw was the underlying game of power and innocence we were trapped in, or how much we needed a racial impasse to play that game.

When I was a boy of about twelve, a white friend of mine told me one day that his uncle, who would be arriving the next day for a visit, was a racist. Excited by the prospect of seeing such a man, I spent the following afternoon hanging around the alley behind my friend's house, watching from a distance as this uncle worked on the engine of his Buick. Yes, here was evil and I was compelled to look upon it. And I saw evil in the sharp angle of his elbow as he pumped his wrench to tighten nuts. I saw it in the blade-sharp crease of his chinos, in the pack of Lucky Strikes that threatened to slip from his shirt pocket as he bent, and in the way his concentration seemed to shut out the human world. He worked neatly and efficiently, wiping his hands constantly, and I decided that evil worked like this.

I felt a compulsion to have this man look upon me so that I could see evil—so that I could see the face of it. But when he noticed me standing beside his toolbox, he said only, "If you're looking for Bobby, I think he went up to the school to play baseball." He smiled nicely and went back to work. I was stunned for a moment, but then I realized that evil could be sly as well, could smile when it wanted to trick you.

Need, especially hidden need, puts a strong pressure on perception, and my need to have this man embody white evil was stronger than any contravening evidence. As a black person you always hear about racists but rarely meet any who will let you know them as such. And I needed to incarnate this odious category of humanity, those people who hated Martin Luther King, Jr., and thought blacks should "go slow" or not at all. So, in my mental dictionary, behind the term "white racist," I inserted this man's likeness. I would think of him and say to myself, "There is no reason for him to hate black people. Only evil explains unmotivated hatred." And this thought soothed me; I felt innocent. If I hated white people, which I did not, at least I had a reason. His evil commanded me to assert in the world the goodness he made me confident of in myself.

In looking at this man I was *seeing for innocence*—a form of seeing that has more to do with one's hidden need for innocence (and power) than with the person or group one is looking at. It is quite possible, for example, that the man I saw that day was not a racist. He did absolutely nothing in my presence to indicate that he was. I invested an entire afternoon in seeing not the man but in seeing my innocence through the man. *Seeing for innocence* is, in this way, the essence of racism—the use of others as a means to our own goodness and superiority.

The loss of innocence has always to do with guilt, Kierkegaard tells us, and it has never been easy for whites to avoid guilt where blacks are concerned. For whites, *seeing for innocence* means seeing themselves and blacks in ways that minimize white guilt. Often this amounts to a kind of white revisionism, as when President Reagan declared himself "color-blind" in matters of race. The President, like many of us, may have aspired to racial color blindness, but few would grant that he ever reached this sublimely guiltless state. His statement clearly revised reality, moved it forward into some heretofore unknown America where all racial determinism would have vanished. I do not think that Ronald Reagan was a racist, as that term is commonly used, but neither do I think that he was capable of seeing color without making attributions, some of which may have been negative—nor am I, or anyone else I've ever met.

So why make such a statement? I think Reagan's claim of color blindness with regard to race was really a claim of racial innocence and guiltlessness—the preconditions for entitlement and power. This was the claim that grounded Reagan's campaign against special entitlement programs—affirmative action, racial quotas, and so on—that black power had won in the sixties. Color blindness was a strategic assumption of innocence that licensed Reagan's use of government power against black power.

I do not object to Reagan's goals in this so much as the presumption of innocence by which he rationalized them. I, too, am strained to defend racial quotas and any affirmative action that supersedes merit. And I believe there was much that Reagan had to offer blacks. His emphasis on traditional American values—individual initiative, self-sufficiency, strong families—offered what I think is the most enduring solution to the demoralization and poverty that continue to widen the gap between blacks and whites in America. Even his de-emphasis of race was reasonable in a society where race only divides. But Reagan's posture of innocence undermined any beneficial interaction he might have had with blacks. For blacks instinctively sense that a claim of racial innocence always precedes a power move against them. Reagan's pretense of innocence made him an adversary and made his quite reasonable message seem vindictive. You cannot be innocent of a man's problem and expect him to listen.

I'm convinced that the secret of Reagan's "Teflon" coating, his personal popularity apart from his policies and actions, was his ability to offer mainstream America a vision of itself as innocent and entitled (unlike Jimmy Carter, who seemed to offer only guilt and obligation). Probably his most far-reaching accomplishment was to reverse somewhat the pattern by which innocence came to be distributed in the sixties, when outsiders were innocent and insiders were guilty. Corporations, the middle class, entrepreneurs, the military—all villains in the sixties—either took on a new innocence in

Reagan's vision or were designated as protectors of innocence. But again, for one man to be innocent, another man must be bad or guilty. Innocence imposes—*demands*—division and conflict, a right/wrong view of the world. And this, I feel, led to the underside of Reagan's achievement. His posture of innocence drew him into a partisanship that undermined the universality of his values. He couldn't sell these values to blacks because he made blacks into the bad guys and outsiders who justified his power. It was humiliating for a black person to like Reagan because Reagan's power was so clearly derived from a distribution of innocence that left blacks with less of it and the white man with more.

Black Americans have had to find a way to handle white society's presumption of racial innocence whenever they have sought to enter the American mainstream. Louis Armstrong's exaggerated smile honored the presumed innocence of white society—*I will not bring you your racial guilt if you will let me play my music*. Ralph Ellison calls this "masking"; I call it bargaining. But whatever it's called, it points to the power of white society to enforce its innocence. I believe this power is greatly diminished today. Society has reformed and transformed—Miles Davis never smiles. Nevertheless, this power has not faded altogether and blacks must still contend with it.

Historically, blacks have handled white society's presumption of innocence in two ways: they have bargained with it, granting white society its innocence in exchange for entry into the mainstream, or they have challenged it, holding that innocence hostage until their demand for entry (or other concessions) was met. A bargainer says, *I already believe you are innocent (good, fair-minded) and have faith that you will prove it*. A challenger says, *If you are innocent, then prove it*. Bargainers *give* in hope of receiving; challengers *withhold* until they receive. Of course, there is risk in both approaches, but in each case the black is negotiating his own self-interest against the presumed racial innocence of the larger society.

Clearly, the most visible black bargainer on the American scene today is Bill Cosby. His television show has been a perfect formula for black bargaining in the eighties. The remarkable Huxtable family—with its doctor/lawyer parent combination, its drug-free, college-bound children, and its wise yet youthful grandparents—is a blackface version of the American dream. Cosby is a subscriber to the American identity, and his subscription confirms his belief in its fair-mindedness. His vast audience knows this, knows that Cosby will never assault their innocence with racial guilt. Racial controversy is all but banished from the show. The Huxtable family never discusses affirmative action.

The bargain Cosby offers his white viewers—*I will confirm your racial innocence if you accept me*—is a good deal for all concerned. Not only does it allow whites to enjoy Cosby's humor with no loss of innocence, but it actually enhances their innocence by implying that race is not the serious problem for blacks that it once was. If anything, the success of this handsome, affluent black family points to the fair-mindedness of whites who, out of their essential goodness, changed society so that black families like the Huxtables could succeed. Whites can watch "The Cosby Show" and feel complimented on a job well done.

The power that black bargainers wield is the power of absolution. On Thursday nights, Cosby, like a priest, absolves his white viewers, forgives and forgets the sins of the past. And for this he is rewarded with an almost sacrosanct status.

Cosby benefits from what might be called the gratitude factor. His continued number-one rating may have something to do with the (white) public's gratitude at being offered a commodity so rare in our time; he tells his white viewers each week that they are okay, and that this black man is not going to challenge them.

When a black bargains, he may invoke the gratitude factor and find himself cherished beyond the measure of his achievement; when he challenges, he may draw the dark projections of whites and become a source of irritation to them. If he moves back and forth between these two options, as I think many blacks do today, he will likely baffle whites. It is difficult for whites either to accept or reject such blacks. It seems to me that Jesse Jackson is such a figure—many whites see Jackson as a challenger by instinct and a bargainer by political ambition. They are uneasy with him, more than a little suspicious. His powerful speech at the 1984 Democratic Convention was a masterpiece of bargaining. In it he offered a King-like vision of what America could be, a vision that presupposed Americans had the fair-mindedness to achieve full equality—an offer in hope of a return. A few days after this speech, looking for rest and privacy at a lodge in Big Sur, he and his wife were greeted with standing ovations three times a day when they entered the dining room for meals. So much about Jackson is deeply American—his underdog striving, his irrepressible faith in himself, the daring of his ambition, and even his stubbornness. These qualities point to his underlying faith that Americans can respond to him despite race, and this faith is a compliment to Americans, an offer of innocence.

But Jackson does not always stick to the terms of his bargain as Cosby does on TV. When he hugs Arafat, smokes cigars with Castro, refuses to repudiate Farrakhan, threatens a boycott of major league baseball or, more recently, talks of "corporate barracudas," "pension-fund socialism," and "economic violence," he looks like a challenger in bargainer's clothing, and his positions on the issues look like familiar protests dressed in white-paper formality. At these times he appears to be revoking the innocence so much else about him seems to offer. The old activist seems to come out of hiding once again to take white innocence hostage until whites prove they deserve to have it. In his candidacy there is a suggestion of protest, a fierce insistence on his *right* to run, that sends whites a message that he may secretly see them as a good bit less than innocent. His dilemma is to appear the bargainer while his campaign itself seems to be a challenge.

There are, of course, other problems that hamper Jackson's bid for the Democratic presidential nomination. He has held no elective office, he is thought too flamboyant and opportunistic by many, there are rather loud whispers of "character" problems. As an individual, he may not be the best test of a black man's chances for winning so high an office. Still, I believe it is the aura of challenge surrounding him that hurts him most. Whether it is right or wrong, fair or unfair, I think no black candidate will have a serious chance at his party's nomination, much less the presidency, until he can convince white Americans that he can be trusted to preserve their sense of racial innocence. Such a candidate will have to use his power of absolution; he will have to flatly forgive and forget. He will have to bargain with white innocence out of genuine belief that it really exists. There can be no faking it. He will have to offer a vision that is passionately raceless, a vision that strongly condemns any form of racial politics. This will require the most courageous kind of leadership, leadership that asks all the people to meet a new standard.

Now the other side of America's racial impasse: How do blacks lay claim to their racial innocence?

The most obvious and unarguable source of black innocence is the victimization that blacks endured for centuries at the hands of a race that insisted on black inferiority as a means to its own innocence and power. Like all victims, what blacks lost in power they gained in innocence—innocence that, in turn, entitled them to pursue power. This was the innocence that fueled the civil rights movement of the sixties and that gave blacks their first real power in American life —victimization metamorphosed into power via innocence. But this formula carries a drawback that I believe is virtually as devastating to blacks today as victimization once was. It is a formula that binds the victim to his victimization by linking his power to his status as a victim. And this, I'm convinced, is the tragedy of black power in America today. It is primarily a victim's power, grounded too deeply in the entitlement derived from past injustice and in the innocence that Western/Christian tradition has always associated with poverty.

Whatever gains this power brings in the short run through political action, it undermines in the long run. Social victims may be collectively entitled, but they are all too often individually demoralized. Since the social victim has been oppressed by society, he comes to feel that his individual life will be improved more by changes in society than by his own initiative. Without realizing it, he makes society rather than himself the agent of change. The power he finds in his victimization may lead him to collective action against society, but it also encourages passivity within the sphere of his personal life.

Not long ago, I saw a television documentary that examined life in Detroit's inner city on the twentieth anniversary of the riots there in which forty-three people were killed. A comparison of the inner city then and now showed a decline in the quality of life. Residents feel less safe, drug trafficking is far worse, crimes by blacks against blacks are more frequent, housing remains substandard, and the teenage pregnancy rate has skyrocketed. Twenty years of decline and demoralization, even as opportunities for blacks to better themselves have increased. This paradox is not peculiar to Detroit. By many measures, the majority of blacks—those not yet in the middle class—are further behind whites today than before the victories of the civil rights movement. But there is a reluctance among blacks to examine this paradox, I think, because it suggests that racial victimization is not our real problem. If conditions have worsened for most of us as racism had receded, then much of the problem must be of our own making. To admit this fully would cause us to lose the innocence we derive from our victimization. And we would jeopardize the entitlement we've always had to challenge society. We are in the odd and self-defeating position in which taking responsibility for bettering ourselves feels like a surrender to white power.

So we have a hidden investment in victimization and poverty. These distressing conditions have been the source of our only real power, and there is an unconscious sort of gravitation toward them, a complaining celebration of them. One sees evidence of this in the near happiness with which certain black leaders recount the horror of Howard Beach, Bensonhurst, and other recent instances of racial tension. As one is saddened by these tragic events, one is also repelled at the way some black leaders—agitated to near hysteria by the scent of victim power inherent in them—leap forward to exploit them as evidence of black innocence and white guilt. It is as though they sense the decline of black victimization as a loss of standing and dive into the middle of these incidents as if they were reservoirs of pure black innocence swollen with potential power.

Seeing for innocence pressures blacks to focus on racism and to neglect the individual initiative that would deliver them from poverty—the only thing that finally delivers *anyone* from poverty. With our eyes on innocence we see racism everywhere and miss opportunity even as we stumble over it. About 70 percent of black students at my university drop out before graduation—a flight from opportunity that racism cannot explain. It is an injustice that whites can see for innocence with more impunity than blacks can. The price whites pay is a certain blindness to themselves. Moreover, for whites seeing for innocence continues to engender the bad faith of a long-disgruntled minority. But the price blacks pay is an ever-escalating poverty that threatens to make the worst off a permanent underclass. Not fair, but real.

Challenging works best for the collective, while bargaining is more the individual's suit. From this point on, the race's advancement will come from the efforts of its individuals. True, some challenging will be necessary for a long time to come. But bargaining is now—today—a way for the black individual to *join* the larger society, to make a place for himself or herself.

"Innocence is ignorance," Kierkegaard says, and if this is so, the claim of innocence amounts to an insistence on ignorance, a refusal to know. In their assertions of innocence both races carve out very functional areas of ignorance for themselves—territories of blindness that license a misguided pursuit of power. Whites gain superiority by not knowing blacks; blacks gain entitlement by not seeing their own responsibility for bettering themselves. The power each race seeks in relation to the other is grounded in a double-edged ignorance of the self as well as of the other.

The original sin that brought us to an impasse at the dinner party I mentioned occurred centuries ago, when it was first decided to exploit racial difference as a means to power. It was a determinism that flowed karmically from this sin that dropped over us like a net that night. What bothered me most was our helplessness. Even the engineer did not know how to go forward. His challenge hadn't worked, and he'd lost the option to bargain. The marriage of race and power depersonalized us, changed us from eight people to six whites and two blacks. The easiest thing was to let silence blanket our situation, our impasse.

I think the civil rights movement in its early and middle years offered the best way out of America's racial impasse: in this society, race must not be a source of advantage or disadvantage for anyone. This is fundamentally a *moral* position, one that seeks to breach the corrupt union of race and power with principles of fairness and human equality: if all men are created equal, then racial difference cannot sanction power. The civil rights movement was conceived for no other reason than to redress that corrupt union, and its guiding insight was that only a moral power based on enduring principles of justice, equality, and freedom could offset the lower impulse in man to exploit race as a means to power. Three hundred years of suffering had driven the point home, and in Montgomery, Little Rock, and Selma, racial power was the enemy and moral power the weapon.

An important difference between genuine and presumed innocence, I believe, is that the former must be earned through sacrifice while the latter is unearned and only veils the quest for privilege. And there was much sacrifice in the early civil rights movement. The Gandhian principle of nonviolent resistance that gave the movement a spiritual center as well as a method of protest demanded sacrifice, a passive offering of the self in the name of justice. A price was paid in terror and lost life, and from this sacrifice came a hard-earned innocence and a credible moral power.

Nonviolent passive resistance is a bargainer's strategy. It assumes the power that is the object of the protest has the genuine innocence to respond morally, and puts the protesters at the mercy of that innocence. I think this movement won so many concessions precisely because of its belief in the capacity of whites to be moral. It did not so much demand that whites change as offer them relentlessly the opportunity to live by their own morality—to attain a true innocence based on the sacrifice of their racial privilege, rather than a false innocence based on presumed racial superiority. Blacks always bargain with or challenge the larger society; but I believe that in the early civil rights years, these forms of negotiation achieved a degree of integrity and genuineness never seen before or since.

In the mid-sixties all this changed. Suddenly a sharp *racial* consciousness emerged to compete with the moral consciousness that had defined the movement up to that point. Whites were no longer welcome in the movement, and a vocal "black power" minority gained dramatic visibility. Increasingly, the movement began to seek racial as well as moral power, and thus it fell into the fundamental contradiction that plagues it to this day. Moral power precludes racial power by denouncing race as a means to power. Now suddenly the movement itself was using race as a means to power and thereby affirming the very union of race and power it was born to redress. In the end, black power can claim no higher moral standing than white power.

It makes no sense to say this shouldn't have happened. The sacrifices that moral power demands are difficult to sustain, and it was inevitable that blacks would tire of these sacrifices and seek a more earthly power. Nevertheless, a loss of genuine innocence and moral power followed. The movement, splintered by a burst of racial militancy in the late sixties, lost its hold on the American conscience and descended more and more to the level of secular interest-group politics. Bargaining and challenging once again became racial rather than moral negotiations.

You hear it asked, why are there no Martin Luther Kings around today? I think one reason is that there are no black leaders willing to resist the seductions of racial power, or to make the sacrifices moral power requires. King understood that racial power subverts moral power, and he pushed the principles of fairness and equality rather than black power because he believed those principles would bring blacks their most complete liberation. He sacrificed race for morality, and his innocence was made genuine by that sacrifice. What made King the most powerful and extraordinary black leader of this century was not his race but his morality.

Black power is a challenge. It grants whites no innocence; it denies their moral capacity and then demands that they be moral. No power can long insist on itself without evoking an opposing power. Doesn't an insistence on black power call up white power? (And could this have something to do with what many are now calling a resurgence of white racism?) I believe that what divided the races at the dinner party I attended, and what divides them in the nation, can only be bridged by an adherence to those moral principles that disallow race as a source of power, privilege, status, or entitlement of any kind. In our age, principles like fairness and equality are ill-defined and all but drowned in relativity. But this is the fault of people, not principles. We keep them muddied because they are the greatest threat to our presumed innocence and our selective ignorance. Moral principles, even when somewhat ambiguous, have the power to assign responsibility and therefore to provide us with knowledge. At the dinner party we were afraid of so severe an accountability.

What both black and white Americans fear are the sacrifices and risks that true racial harmony demands. This fear is the measure of our racial chasm. And though fear always seeks a thousand justifications, none is ever good enough, and the problems we run from only remain to haunt us. It would be right to suggest courage as an antidote to fear, but the glory of the word might only intimidate us into more fear. I prefer the word effort—relentless effort, moral effort. What I like most about this word are its connotations of everydayness, earnestness, and practical sacrifice. No matter how badly it might have gone for us that warm summer night, we should have talked. We should have made the effort.

2

Race-Holding

■

I am a fortyish, middle-class, black American male with a teaching position at a large state university in California. I have owned my own home for more than ten years, as well as the two cars that are the minimal requirement for life in California. And I will confess to a moderate strain of yuppie hedonism. Year after year my two children are the sole representatives of their race in their classrooms, a fact they sometimes have difficulty remembering. We are the only black family in our suburban neighborhood, and even this claim to specialness is diminished by the fact that my wife is white. I think we are called an "integrated" family, though no one has ever used the term with me. For me to be among large numbers of blacks requires conscientiousness and a long car ride, and in truth, I have not been very conscientious lately. Though I was raised in an all-black community just south of Chicago, I only occasionally feel nostalgia for such places. Trips to the barbershop now and then usually satisfy this need, though recently, in the interest of convenience, I've taken to letting my wife cut my hair.

I see in people's eyes from time to time, and hear often in the media, what amounts to a judgment of people like myself: You have moved into the great amorphous middle class and lost your connection to your people and your cultural roots. You have become a genuine invisible man. This is a judgment with many obvious dimensions, many arrows of guilt. But, in essence, it charges me with selfishness and inauthenticity.

At one point I romanticized my situation, thought of myself as a marginal man. The seductive imagery of alienation supported me in this. But in America today racial marginality is hard to sell as the stuff of tragedy. The position brings with it an ugly note of self-insistence that annoys people in a society that is, at least officially, desegregated.

For better or worse, I'm not very marginal. In my middle-American world I see people like myself everywhere. We nod coolly at stoplights, our eyes connect for an awkward instant in shopping malls, we hear about one another from our white friends. "Have you met the new doctor at the hospital . . . the engineer at IBM . . . the new professor in history?" The black middle class is growing. We are often said to be sneaking or slipping or creeping unnoticed into the middle class, as though images of stealth best characterized our movement. I picture a kind of underground railroad, delivering us in the dead of night from the inner city to the suburbs.

But even if we aren't very marginal, we are very shy with one another, at least until we've had a chance to meet privately and take our readings. When we first meet, we experience a trapped feeling, as if we had walked into a cage of racial expectations that would rob us of our individuality by reducing us to an exclusively racial dimension. We are a threat, at first, to one another's uniqueness. I have seen the same well-dressed black woman in the supermarket for more than a year now. We do not speak, and we usually pretend not to see each other. But, when we turn a corner suddenly and find ourselves staring squarely into each other's eyes, her face freezes and she moves on. I believe she is insisting that both of us be more than black—that we interact only when we have a reason other than the mere fact of our race. Her chilliness enforces a priority I agree with—individuality over group identity.

But I believe I see something else in this woman that I also see in myself and in many other middle-class blacks. It is a kind of race fatigue, a deep weariness with things racial, which comes from the fact that our lives are more integrated than they have ever been before. Race does not determine our fates as powerfully as it once did, which means it is not the vital personal concern it once was. Before the sixties, race set the boundaries of black life. Now, especially for middle-class blacks, it is far less a factor, though we don't always like to admit it. Blacks still suffer from racism, so we must be concerned, but this need to be concerned with what is not so personally urgent makes for race fatigue.

I have a friend who did poorly in the insurance business for years. "People won't buy insurance from a black man," he always said. Two years ago another black man and a black woman joined his office. Almost immediately both did twice the business my friend was doing, with the same largely white client base.

Integration shock is essentially the shock of being suddenly accountable on strictly personal terms. It occurs in situations that disallow race as an excuse for personal shortcomings and it therefore exposes vulnerabilities that previously were hidden. One response to such shock is to face up to the self-confrontation it brings and then to act on the basis of what we learn about ourselves. After some struggle, my friend was able to do this. He completely revised his sales technique, asked himself some hard questions about his motivation, and resolved to work harder.

But when one lacks the courage to face oneself fully, a fear of hidden vulnerabilities triggers a fright-flight response to integration shock. Instead of admitting that racism has declined, we argue all the harder that it is still alive and more insidious than ever. We hold race up to shield us from what we do not want to see in ourselves. My friend did this at first, saying that the two blacks in this office were doing better than he was because they knew how to "kiss white ass." Here he was *race-holding*, using race to keep from looking at himself.

Recently I read an article in the local paper that explored the question of whether blacks could feel comfortable living in the largely white Silicon Valley. The article focused on a black family that had been living for more than a decade in Saratoga, a very well-to-do white community. Their neighborhood, their children's schools, their places of employment, their shopping areas and parks—their entire physical environment—were populated by affluent whites. Yet during the interview the wife said they had made two firm rules for their children: that they go to all-black colleges back east and that they do "no dating outside the race, period."

I have pushed enough black history and culture on my own children to be able to identify with the impulse behind the first of these rules. Black children in largely white situations must understand and appreciate their cultural background. But the rigidity of these rules, not to mention the rules themselves, points to more than a concern with transmitting heritage or gaining experience with other blacks. Rigidity arises from fear and self-doubt. These people, I believe, were afraid of something.

What was striking to me about their rules, especially the one prohibiting interracial dating, was their tone of rejection. The black parents seemed as determined to reject the white world as to embrace the black one. Why? I would say because of integration shock. Their integrated lives have opened up vulnerabilities they do not wish to face. But what vulnerabilities? In this case, I think, a particularly embarrassing one. On some level, I suspect, they doubt whether they are as good as the white people who live around them. You cannot be raised in a culture that was for centuries committed to the notion of your inferiority and not have some doubt in this regard—doubt that is likely to be aggravated most in integrated situations. So the rejecting tone of their rules is self-protective: *I will reject you before you have a chance to reject me.* But all of this is covered over by race. The high value of racial pride is invoked to shield them from a doubt that they are afraid to acknowledge. Unacknowledged, this doubt gains a negative power inside the personality that expresses itself in the rigidity and absolutism of their rules. Repressed fears tend always to escalate their campaign for our attention by pushing us further and further into irrationality and rigidity.

The refusal to see something unflattering in ourselves always triggers the snap from race fatigue to race-holding. And once that happens, we are caught, like this family, in a jumble of racial ironies. The parents in Saratoga, who have chosen to live integrated lives, impose a kind of segregation on their children. Rules that would be racist in the mouth of any white

person are created and enforced with pride. Their unexamined
self-doubt also leaves them unable to exploit fully the freedom
they have attained. Race fatigue makes them run to a place
like Saratoga, but integration shock makes them hold race
protectively. They end up clinging to what they've run from.

Once race-holding is triggered by fear, it ensnares us in a
web of self-defeating attitudes that end up circumventing the
new freedoms we've won over the past several decades. I have
seen its corrosive effects in my own life and in the lives of
virtually every black person I've known. Some are only mildly
touched by it, while others seem incapacitated by it. But
race-holding is as unavoidable as defensiveness itself, and I
am convinced that it is one of the most debilitating, yet
unrecognized, forces in black life today.

I define a *holding* as any self-description that serves to
justify or camouflage a person's fears, weaknesses, and in-
adequacies. Holdings are the little and big exaggerations,
distortions, and lies about ourselves that prop us up and let
us move along the compromised paths we follow. They develop
to defend against threats to our self-esteem, threats that make
us feel vulnerable and that plant a seed of fear. This fear can
work like wind on a brushfire, spreading self-doubt far beyond
what the initial threat would warrant, so that we become even
more weakened and more needy of holdings. Since holdings
justify our reticence and cowardice, they are usually ex-
pressed in the form of high belief or earthy wisdom. A man
whose business fails from his own indifference holds an image
of himself as a man too honest to be a good businessman—
a self-description that draws a veil over his weakness.

For some years I have noticed that I can walk into any of
my classes on the first day of the semester, identify the black

students, and be sadly confident that on the last day of the semester a disproportionate number of them will be at the bottom of the class, far behind any number of white students of equal or even lesser native ability. More to the point, they will have performed far beneath their own native ability. Self-fulfilling prophesy theory says that their schools have always expected them to do poorly, and that they have internalized this message and *done* poorly. But this deterministic theory sees blacks only as victims, without any margin of choice. It cannot fully explain the poor performances of these black students because it identifies only the forces that *pressure* them to do poorly. By overlooking the margin of choice open to them, this theory fails to recognize the degree to which they are responsible for their own poor showing. (The irony of this oversight is that it takes the power for positive change away from the students and puts it in the hands of the very institutions that failed them in the first place.)

The theory of race-holding is based on the assumption that a margin of choice is always open to blacks (even slaves had some choice). And it tries to make clear the mechanisms by which we relinquish that choice in the name of race. With the decline in racism the margin of black choice has greatly expanded, which is probably why race-holding is so much more visible today than ever before. But anything that prevents us from exploiting our new freedom to the fullest is now as serious a barrier to us as racism once was.

The self-fulfilling prophesy theory is no doubt correct that black students, like the ones I regularly see, internalize a message of inferiority that they receive from school and the larger society around them. But the relevant question in the 1990s is why they *choose* to internalize this view of themselves. Why do they voluntarily perceive themselves as inferior? We can talk about the weakened black family and countless other scars of oppression and poverty. And certainly these things have much to do with the image these students have of themselves. But they do not fully explain this self-image because none of them entirely eliminates the margin of choice that remains open. Choice lives in even the most blighted circumstances, and it certainly lives in the lives of these black college students.

I think they *choose* to believe in their inferiority, not to fulfill society's prophesy about them, but for the comforts and rationalizations their racial "inferiority" affords them. They hold their race to evade individual responsibility. Their margin of choice scares them, as it does all people. They are naturally intimidated by that eternal tussle between the freedom to act and the responsibility we must take for our actions. To some extent all of us balk in the face of this. The difference is that these students use their race to conceal the fact that they are balking. Their "inferiority" shields them from having to see that they are afraid of all-out competition with white students. And it isn't even an honest inferiority. I don't think they really believe it. It is a false inferiority, *chosen* over an honest and productive confrontation with white students and with their real fears—a strategy that allows them to stay comfortably on the sidelines in a university environment that all but showers them with opportunity.

"I'm doing okay for a black student," a student once told me. "I'm doing well considering where I came from," I have told myself. Race allows us both to hide from the real question, which is, "Am I doing what I can, considering my talents and energies?"

I see all of this as pretty much a subconscious process, fear working on a subterranean level to let us reduce our margin of choice in the name of race. Consciously, we tell ourselves that we are only identifying with our race, but fear bloats our racial identity to an unnatural size and then uses it as cover for its subversive work. The more severe the integration shock, the more fear cover is needed.

Doesn't race enhance individuality? I think it does, but only when individuality is nurtured and developed apart from race. The race-holder, inside the bubble of his separate self, feels inadequate or insecure and then seeks reassurance through race. When, instead, a sense of self arises from individual achievement and self-realization. When self-esteem is established apart from race, then racial identity can only enhance because it is no longer needed for any other purpose.

The word *individualism* began to connote selfishness and even betrayal for many blacks during the sixties. Individualism was seen as a threat to the solidarity blacks needed during those years of social confrontation. Despite the decline in racism, these connotations have lingered. Race-holding keeps them alive because they serve the race-holder's need to exaggerate the importance of race as well as to justify a fear of individual responsibility. Race-holding makes fluid the boundary between race and self, group and individual identity, so that race can swing over at a moment's notice and fill in where fears leave a vacuum.

This is a worse problem than is at first apparent because the individual is the seat of all energy, creativity, motivation, and power. We are most strongly motivated when we want something for ourselves. When our personal wants are best achieved through group action, as in the civil rights movement, we lend our energy to the group, and it becomes as strong as the sum of our energies. When the need for group action recedes, more energy is available to us as individuals. But race-holding intercedes here by affixing the race-holder too tightly to this racial identity and by causing him to see the locus of power in race rather than in himself. In this way race-holding corrupts the greatest source of power and strength available to blacks—the energy latent in our personal desires.

One of my favorite passages in Ralph Ellison's *Invisible Man* is his description of the problem of blacks as

> not actually one of creating the uncreated con- science of [our] race, but of creating the *uncreated features of [our] face*. Our task is that of making ourselves individuals. . . . We create the race by creating ourselves and then to our great astonish- ment we will have created something far more important: we will have created a culture.

These lines hold up well, more than thirty years after they were written. They seem to suggest a kind of Adam Smith vision of culture: When the individual makes himself, he makes culture. An "invisible hand" uses individual effort to define and broaden culture. In the 1990s we blacks are more than ever in a position where our common good will best be served by the determined pursuit of our most personal as- pirations.

I think the means to this, and the answer to race-holding generally, is personal responsibility, a source of great power that race-holding does its best to conceal.

Some years ago I made a mistake at a neighbor's cocktail

party that taught me something about personal responsibility. I went to the party for the thinnest of reasons—mere politeness—though the afternoon was hot and I was already in a peevish mood. The event would have been problematic even if I weren't the only black at the party. But I was, and on this afternoon I *chose* to make note of the fact, though it was hardly a new experience for me. As I strolled around the sun-baked patio, avoiding people more than engaging them, I held this fact more and more tightly until I came to believe it had a profound meaning I needed to understand. After a while I decided that others needed to understand it, too.

In the sixties, blacks and white liberals often engaged in something that might be called the harangue-flagellation ritual. Blacks felt anger, white liberals felt guilt, and when they came together, blacks would vent their anger by haranguing the whites, who often allowed themselves to be scourged as a kind of penance. The "official" black purpose of this rite was to "educate" whites on the issue of race, and in the sixties this purpose may sometimes have been served. But in the eighties, after a marked decline in racism and two decades of consciousness-raising, the rite had become both anachronistic and, I think, irresponsible. Nevertheless, it suited my mood on this hot afternoon, so I retrieved it from its dusty bin and tried to make it fashionable again.

A woman at the party said how much she liked Jesse Jackson's rhetorical style. Was "style" the only thing she liked? I asked, with an edge to my voice. The woman gave me a curious and exasperated look, but I pushed on anyway. Soon I was lecturing the six or seven people around me: I told them that racism had been driven underground in the sixties and seventies, where more insidious strategies for foiling the possibilities of black people had evolved. I pointed to the black unemployment rate, the continued segregation of many schools, housing discrimination, and so on. Soon I saw that the old harangue-flagellation ritual was firmly back in place. I was shaming these people, and they nodded at what I said in a way that gratified me.

But at home that night I felt a stinging shame, and even weeks later the thought of that afternoon made me cringe. Eventually I saw why. For one thing, I was trading on my race with those people, using the very thing I claimed to be so concerned with to buy my way out of certain anxieties. Like the Saratoga family, I was race-holding in response to the integration shock I felt in this integrated situation. I had begun to feel vulnerable, and I hit those people with race before they could hit me with it. My vulnerabilities, of course, were essentially the same as the Saratoga family's. On some level I doubted myself in relation to these whites, and my insecurities drove me into an offense that was really a defense. The shame I began to feel, though I could not identify it at the time, was essentially the shame of cowardice. I felt as though I'd run away from something and used race to cover my tracks.

This shame had another dimension that was even more humiliating than the cowardice I had felt. On that patio I was complaining to white people, beseeching them to see how badly blacks were still treated, and I was gratified to see their heads nod as though they understood. My voice contained no audible whine, but at least some of what I said amounted to a whine. And this is what put the sting in my shame. Cowardice was a common enough fault, but whining was quite another thing.

The race-holder whines, or complains indiscriminately, not because he seeks redress but because he seeks the status of victim, a status that excuses him from what he fears. A victim is not responsible for his condition, and by claiming a victim's status the race-holder gives up the sense of personal responsibility he needs to better his condition. His unseen purpose is to hide rather than fight, so the anger and, more importantly, the energy that real racism breeds in him is squandered in self-serving complaint. The price he pays for the false comfort of his victim's status is a kind of impotence.

The difference between the race-holder who merely complains and the honest protester is that the latter keeps the responsibility for his condition in his own hands. The honest protester may be victimized, but he is not solely a victim. He thinks of himself as fully human and asks only that the rules of the game be made fair. Through fairness, rather than entitlement, he retains his personal responsibility and the power that grows out of it. But he also understands that he must keep this responsibility whether or not society is fair. His purpose is to realize himself, to live the fullest possible life, and he is responsible for this, like all men, regardless of how society treats him.

Personal responsibility is the brick and mortar of power. The responsible person knows that the quality of his life is something that he will have to make inside the limits of his fate. Some of these limits he can push back, some he cannot, but in any case the quality of his life will pretty much reflect the quality of his efforts. When this link between well-being and action is truly accepted, the result is power. With this understanding and the knowledge that he is responsible, a person can see his margin of choice. He can choose and act, and choose and act again, without illusion. He can create himself and make himself felt in the world. Such a person has power.

I was neither responsible nor powerful as I stood on my neighbor's patio complaining about racism to these polite people. In effect I was asking them to be fully responsible for something that blacks and whites *share* responsibility for. Whites must guarantee a free and fair society. But blacks must be responsible for actualizing their own lives. If I had said this to the people at the party, maybe they would have gone away with a clearer sense of their own responsibilities. But I never considered it because the real goal of my complaining was to disguise a fear I didn't want to acknowledge.

The barriers to black progress in America today are clearly as much psychological as they are social or economic. We have suffered as much as any group in human history, and if this suffering has ennobled us, it has also wounded us and pushed us into defensive strategies that are often self-defeating. But we haven't fully admitted this to ourselves. The psychological realm is murky, frightening, and just plain embarrassing. And a risk is involved in exploring it: the risk of discovering the ways in which we contribute to, if not create, the reality in which we live. Denial, avoidance, and repression intervene to save us from this risk. But, of course, they only energize what is repressed with more and more negative power, so that we are victimized as much by our own buried fears as by racism.

In the deepest sense, the long struggle of blacks in America has always been a struggle to retrieve our full humanity. But now the reactive stance we adopted to defend ourselves against oppression binds us to the same racial views that oppressed us in the first place. Snakelike, our defense has turned on us. I think it is now the last barrier to the kind of self-possession that will give us our full humanity, and we must overcome it ourselves.

3

Being Black and Feeling Blue

Black Hesitation on the Brink

In the early seventies when I was in graduate school, I went out for a beer late one afternoon with another black graduate student whom I'd only known casually before. This student was older than I—a stint in the army had interrupted his education—and he had the reputation of being bright and savvy, of having applied street smarts to the business of getting through graduate school. I suppose I was hoping for what would be called today a little mentoring. But it is probably not wise to drink with someone when you are enamored of his reputation, and it was not long before we stumbled into a moment that seemed to transform him before my very eyes. I asked him what he planned to do when he finished his Ph.D., fully expecting to hear of high aspirations matched with shrewd perceptions on how to reach them. But before he could think, he said with a kind of exhausted sincerity,

"Man, I just want to hold on, get a job that doesn't work me too hard, and do a lot of fishing." Was he joking, I asked. "Hell, no," he said with exaggerated umbrage. "I'm not into it like the white boys. I don't need what they need."

I will call this man Henry and report that, until five or six years ago when I lost track of him, he was doing exactly as he said he would do. With much guile and little ambition he had moved through a succession of low-level administrative and teaching jobs, mainly in black studies programs. Of course, it is no crime to just "hold on," and it is hardly a practice limited to blacks. Still, in Henry's case there was truly a troubling discrepancy between his ambition and a fine intelligence recognized by all who knew him. But in an odd way this intelligence was more lateral than vertical, and I would say that it was rechanneled by a certain unseen fear into the business of merely holding on. It would be easy to say that Henry had simply decided on life in a slower lane than he was capable of traveling in, or that he was that rare person who had achieved ambitionless contentment. But if this was so, Henry would have had wisdom rather than savvy, and he would not have felt the need to carry himself with more self-importance than his station justified. I don't think Henry was uninterested in ambition; I think he was afraid of it.

It is certainly true that there is a little of Henry in most people. My own compulsion to understand him informs me that I must have seen many elements of myself in him. And though I'm sure he stands for a universal human blockage, I also believe that there is something in the condition of being black in America that makes the kind of hesitancy he represents one of black America's most serious and debilitating problems. As Henry reached the very brink of expanded opportunity, with Ph.D. in hand, he diminished his ambition almost as though his degree delivered him to a kind of semiretirement. I don't think blacks in general have any illusions about semiretirement, but I do think that, as a group, we have hesitated on the brink of new opportunities that we made enormous sacrifices to win for ourselves. The evidence of this lies in one of the most tragic social ironies of late twentieth-century American life: as black Americans have gained in equality and opportunity, we have also declined in relation to whites, so that by many socioeconomic measures we are further behind whites today than before the great victories of the civil rights movement. By one report, even the black middle class, which had made great gains in the seventies, began to lose ground to its white counterpart in the eighties. Most distressing of all, the black underclass continues to expand rather than shrink.

Of course, I don't suggest that Henry's peculiar inertia singularly explains social phenomena so complex and tragic. I do believe, however, that blacks in general are susceptible to the same web of attitudes and fears that kept Henry beneath his potential, and that our ineffectiveness in taking better advantage of our greater opportunity has much to do with this. I think there is a specific form of racial anxiety that all blacks are vulnerable to that can, in situations where we must engage the mainstream society, increase our self-doubt and undermine our confidence so that we often back away from the challenges that, if taken, would advance us. I believe this hidden racial anxiety may well now be the strongest barrier to our full participation in the American mainstream; that it is as strong or stronger even than the discrimination we still face. To examine this racial anxiety, allow me first to look at how the Henry was born in me.

Until the sixth grade, I attended a segregated school in a small working-class black suburb of Chicago. The school was a dumping ground for teachers with too little competence or mental stability to teach in the white school in our district. In 1956, when I entered the sixth grade, I encountered a new addition to the menagerie of misfits that was our faculty—an ex-Marine whose cruelty was suggested during our first lunch hour when he bit the cap off his Coke bottle and spit it into the wastebasket. Looking back I can see that there was no interesting depth to the cruelty he began to show us almost immediately—no consumptive hatred, no intelligent malevolence. Although we were all black and he was white, I don't think he was even particularly racist. He had obviously needed us to like him though he had no faith that we would. He ran the class like a gang leader, picking favorites one day and banishing them the next. And then there was a permanent pool of outsiders, myself among them, who were made to carry the specific sins that he must have feared most in himself.

The sin I was made to carry was the sin of stupidity. I misread a sentence on the first day of school, and my fate was sealed. He made my stupidity a part of the classroom lore, and very quickly I in fact became stupid. I all but lost the ability to read and found the simplest math beyond me. His punishments for my errors rose in meanness until one day he ordered me to pick up all of the broken glass on the playground with my bare hands. Of course, this would have to be the age of the pop bottle, and there were sections of this playground that glared like a mirror in sunlight. After half an hour's labor I sat down on strike, more out of despair than rebellion.

Again, cruelty was no more than a vibration in this man,

and so without even a show of anger he commandeered a
bicycle, handed it to an eighth-grader—one of his lieu-
tenants—and told the boy to run me around the school
grounds "until he passes out." The boy was also given a
baseball bat to "use on him when he slows down." I ran two
laps, about a mile, and then pretended to pass out. The
eighth-grader knew I was playing possum but could not bring
himself to hit me and finally rode off. I exited the school yard
through an adjoining cornfield and never returned.

I mention this experience as an example of how one's innate
capacity for insecurity is expanded and deepened, of how a
disbelieving part of the self is brought to life and forever
joined to the believing self. As children we are all wounded
in some way and to some degree by the wild world we encounter. From these wounds a disbelieving *anti-self* is born,
an internal antagonist and saboteur that embraces the world's
negative view of us, that believes our wounds are justified by
our own unworthiness, and that entrenches itself as a lifelong
voice of doubt. This anti-self is a hidden aggressive force that
scours the world for fresh evidence of our unworthiness. When
the believing self announces its aspirations, the anti-self always argues against them, but never on their merits (this is
a healthy function of the believing self). It argues instead
against our worthiness to pursue these aspirations and, by its
lights, we are never worthy of even our smallest dreams. The
mission of the anti-self is to deflate the believing self and,
thus, draw it down into inertia, passivity, and faithlessness.

The anti-self is the unseen agent of low self-esteem; it
is a catalytic energy that tries to induce low self-esteem in
the believing self as though it were the complete truth of the
personality. The anti-self can only be contained by the
strength of the believing self, and this is where one's early

environment becomes crucial. If the childhood environment is stable and positive, the family whole and loving, the schools good, the community safe, then the believing self will be reinforced and made strong. If the family is shattered, the schools indifferent, the neighborhood a mine field of dangers, the anti-self will find evidence everywhere with which to deflate the believing self.

This does not mean that a bad childhood cannot be overcome. But it does mean—as I have experienced and observed—that one's *capacity* for self-doubt and self-belief are roughly the same from childhood on, so that years later when the believing self may have strengthened enough to control the anti-self, one will still have the same capacity for doubt whether or not one has the *actual* doubt. I think it is this struggle between our capacities for doubt and belief that gives our personalities one of their peculiar tensions and, in this way, marks our character.

My own anti-self was given new scope and power by this teacher's persecution, and it was so successful in deflating my believing self that I secretly vowed never to tell my parents what was happening to me. The anti-self had all but sold my believing self on the idea that I was stupid, and I did not want to feel that shame before my parents. It was my brother who finally told them, and his disclosure led to a boycott that closed the school and eventually won the dismissal of my teacher and several others. But my anti-self transformed even this act of rescue into a cause of shame—if there wasn't something wrong with me, why did I have to be rescued? The anti-self follows only the logic of self-condemnation.

But there was another dimension to this experience that my anti-self was only too happy to seize upon. It was my race that landed me in this segregated school and, as many adults made clear to me, my persecution followed a timeless pattern of racial persecution. The implications of this were rich food for the anti-self—my race was so despised that it had to be segregated; as a black my education was so unimportant that even unbalanced teachers without college degrees were adequate; ignorance and cruelty that would be intolerable in a classroom of whites was perfectly all right in a classroom of blacks. The anti-self saw no injustice in any of this, but instead took it all as confirmation of a racial inferiority that it could now add to the well of personal doubt I already had. When the adults thought they were consoling me—*"Don't worry. They treat all blacks this way"*—they were also deepening the wound and expanding my capacity for doubt.

And this is the point. The condition of being black in America means that one will likely endure more wounds to one's self-esteem than others and that the capacity for self-doubt born of these wounds will be compounded and expanded by the black race's reputation of inferiority. The anti-self will most likely have more ammunition with which to deflate the believing self and its aspirations. And the universal human struggle to have belief win out over doubt will be more difficult.

More than difficult, it is also made inescapable by the fact of skin color, which, in America, works as a visual invocation of the problem. Black skin has more dehumanizing stereotypes associated with it than any other skin color in America, if not the world. When a black presents himself in an integrated situation, he knows that his skin alone may bring these stereotypes to life in the minds of those he meets and that he, as an individual, may be diminished by his race before he has a chance to reveal a single aspect of his personality. By the symbology of color that operates in our culture, black

kin accuses him of inferiority. Under the weight of this accusation, a black will almost certainly doubt himself on some
level and to some degree. The ever-vigilant anti-self will grab
this racial doubt and mix it into the pool of personal doubt,
so that when a black walks into an integrated situation—a
largely white college campus, an employment office, a business lunch—he will be vulnerable to the entire realm of his
self-doubt before a single word is spoken.

This constitutes an intense and lifelong racial vulnerability
and anxiety for blacks. Even though a white American may
have been wounded more than a given black, and therefore
have a larger realm of inner doubt, his white skin, with its
connotations of privilege and superiority, will actually help
protect him from that doubt and from the undermining power
of his anti-self, at least in relations with blacks. In fact, the
larger the realm of doubt, the more he may be tempted to
rely on his white skin for protection from it. Certainly in every
self-avowed white racist, whether businessman or member of
the Klan, there is a huge realm of self-contempt and doubt
that hides behind the mythology of white skin. The mere need
to pursue self-esteem through skin color suggests there is no
faith that it can be pursued any other way. But if skin color
offers whites a certain false esteem and impunity, it offers
blacks vulnerability.

This vulnerability begins for blacks with the recognition
that we belong, quite simply, to the most despised race in
the human community of races. To be a member of such a
group in a society where all others gain an impunity by merely
standing in relation to us is to live with a relentless openness
to diminishment and shame. By the devious logic of the anti-
self, one cannot be open to such diminishment without in
fact being inferior and therefore deserving of diminishment.

For the anti-self, the charge verifies the crime, so that racial vulnerability itself is evidence of inferiority. In this sense, the anti-self is an internalized racist, our own subconscious bigot, that conspires with society to diminish us.

So when blacks enter the mainstream, they are not only vulnerable to society's racism but also to the racist within. This internal racist is not restricted by law, morality, or social decorum. It cares nothing about civil rights and equal opportunity. It is the self-doubt born of the original wound of racial oppression, and its mission is to establish the justice of that wound and shackle us with doubt.

Of course, the common response to racial vulnerability, as to most vulnerabilities, is denial—the mind's mechanism for ridding itself of intolerable possibilities. For blacks to acknowledge a vulnerability to inferiority anxiety, in the midst of a society that has endlessly accused us of being inferior, feels nothing less than intolerable—as if we were agreeing with the indictment against us. But denial is not the same as eradication, since it only gives unconscious life to what is intolerable to our consciousness. Denial reassigns rather than vanquishes the terror of racial vulnerability. This reassignment only makes the terror stronger by making it unknown. When we deny, we always create a dangerous area of self-ignorance, an entire territory of the self that we cannot afford to know. Without realizing it, we begin to circumscribe our lives by avoiding those people and situations that might breach our denial and force us to see consciously what we fear. Though the denial of racial vulnerability is a human enough response, I think it also makes our public discourse on race circumspect and unproductive, since we cannot talk meaningfully about problems we are afraid to name.

Denial is a refusal of painful self-knowledge. When someone or something threatens to breach this refusal, we receive an unconscious shock of the very vulnerability we have denied—a shock that often makes us retreat and more often makes us intensify our denial. When blacks move into integrated situations or face challenges that are new for blacks, the myth of black inferiority is always present as a *condition* of the situation, and as such it always threatens to breach our denial of racial vulnerability. It also threatens to make us realize consciously what is intolerable to us—that we have some anxiety about inferiority. We feel this threat unconsciously as a shock of racial doubt delivered by the racist anti-self (always the inner voice of the myth of black inferiority). Consciously, we feel this shock as a sharp discomfort or a desire to retreat from the situation. Almost always we will want to intensify our denial.

I will call this *integration shock*, since it occurs most powerfully when blacks leave their familiar world and enter the mainstream. Integration shock and denial are mutual intensifiers. The stab of racial doubt that integration shock delivers is a pressure to intensify denial, and a more rigid denial means the next stab of doubt will be more threatening and therefore more intense. The symbiosis of these two forces is, I believe, one of the reasons black Americans have become preoccupied with racial pride, almost to the point of obsession over the past twenty-five or so years. With more exposure to the mainstream, we have endured more integration shock, more jolts of inferiority anxiety. And, I think, we have often responded with rather hyperbolic claims of black pride by which we deny that anxiety. In this sense, our self-consciousness around pride, our need to make a point of it, is, to a degree, a form of denial. Pride becomes denial when it ceases to reflect self-esteem quietly and begins to compensate loudly for unacknowledged inner doubt. Here it also becomes dangerous since it prevents us from confronting and overcoming that doubt.

I think the most recent example of black pride-as-denial is the campaign (which seems to have been launched by a committee) to add yet another name to the litany of names that blacks have given themselves over the past century. Now we are to be African-Americans instead of, or in conjunction with, being black Americans. This self-conscious reaching for pride through nomenclature suggests nothing so much as a despair over the possibility of gaining the less conspicuous pride that follows real advancement. In its invocation of the glories of a remote African past and its wistful suggestion of homeland, this name denies the doubt black Americans have about their contemporary situation in America. There is no element of self-confrontation in it, no facing of real racial vulnerabilities, as there was with the name "black." I think "black" easily became the name of preference in the sixties, precisely because it was not a denial but a confrontation of inferiority anxiety, with the shame associated with the color black. There was honest self-acceptance in this name, and I think it diffused much of our vulnerability to the shame of color. Even between blacks, "black" is hardly the drop-dead fighting word it was when I was a child. Possibly we are ready now for a new name, but I think "black" has been our most powerful name yet because it so frankly called out our shame and doubt and helped us (and others) to accept ourselves. In the name "African-American" there is too much false neutralization of doubt, too much looking away from the caldron of our own experience. It is a euphemistic name that hides us even from ourselves.

I think blacks have been more preoccupied with pride over the past twenty-five years because we have been more exposed to integration shock since the 1964 Civil Rights Act made equal opportunity the law of the land (if not quite the full reality of the land). Ironically, it was the inequality of opportunity and all the other repressions of legal segregation that buffered us from our racial vulnerability. In a segregated society we did not have the same accountability to the charge of racial inferiority since we were given little opportunity to disprove the charge. It was the opening up of opportunity—anti-discrimination laws, the social programs of the Great Society, equal opportunity guidelines and mandates, fair housing laws, affirmative action, and so on—that made us individually and collectively more accountable to the myth of black inferiority and therefore more racially vulnerable.

This vulnerability has increased in the same proportion that our freedom and opportunity have increased. The exhilaration of new freedom is always followed by a shock of accountability. Whatever unresolved doubt follows the oppressed into greater freedom will be inflamed since freedom always carries a burden of proof, always throws us back on ourselves. And freedom, even imperfect freedom, makes blacks a brutal proposition: if you're not inferior, prove it. This is the proposition that shocks us and makes us vulnerable to our underworld of doubt. The whispers of the racist anti-self are far louder in the harsh accountability of freedom than in subjugation, where the oppressor is so entirely to blame.

The bitter irony of all this is that our doubt and the hesitancy it breeds now help limit our progress in America almost as systematically as segregation once did. Integration shock gives the old boundaries of legal segregation a regenerative power. To avoid the shocks of doubt that come from entering the mainstream, or plunging more deeply into it, we often pull back at precisely those junctures where segregation once pushed us back. In this way we duplicate the conditions of our oppression and reenact our role as victims even in the midst of far greater freedom and far less victimization. Certainly there is still racial discrimination in America, but I believe that the unconscious replaying of our oppression is now the greatest barrier to our full equality.

The way in which integration shock regenerates the old boundaries of segregation for blacks is most evident in three tendencies—the tendency to minimalize or avoid real opportunities, to withhold effort in areas where few blacks have achieved, and to self-segregate in integrated situations.

If anything, it is the presence of new opportunities in society that triggers integration shock. If opportunity is a chance to succeed, it is also a chance to fail. The vulnerability of blacks to hidden inferiority anxiety makes failure a much more forbidding prospect. If a black pursues an opportunity in the mainstream—opens a business, goes up for a challenging job or difficult promotion—and fails, that failure can be used by the anti-self to confirm both personal and racial inferiority. The diminishment and shame will tap an impersonal, as well as personal, source of doubt. When a white fails, he alone fails. His doubt is strictly personal, which gives him more control over the failure. He can discover *his* mistakes, learn the reasons *he* made them, and try again. But the black, laboring under the myth of inferiority, will have this impersonal, culturally determined doubt with which to contend. This form of doubt robs him of a degree of control over his failure since he alone cannot eradicate the cultural myth that stings him. There will be a degree of impenetrability to his failure that will constitute an added weight of doubt.

The effect of this is to make mainstream opportunity more intimidating and risky for blacks. This is made worse in that blacks, owing to past and present deprivations, may come to the mainstream in the first place with a lower stock of self-esteem. High risk and low self-esteem is hardly the best combination with which to tackle the challenges of a highly advanced society in which others have been blessed by history with very clear advantages. Under these circumstances, opportunity can seem more like a chance to fail than a chance to succeed. All this makes for a kind of opportunity aversion that I think was behind the hesitancy I saw in Henry, in myself, and in other blacks of all class backgrounds. It is also, I believe, one of the reasons for the sharp decline in the number of black students entering college, even as many colleges launch recruiting drives to attract more black students.

This aversion to opportunity generates a way of seeing that minimalizes opportunity to the point where it can be ignored. In black communities the most obvious entrepreneurial opportunities are routinely ignored. It is often outsiders or the latest wave of immigrants who own the shops, restaurants, cleaners, gas stations, and even the homes and apartments. Education is a troubled area in black communities for numerous reasons, but certainly one of them is that many black children are not truly imbued with the idea that learning is virtually the same as opportunity. Schools—even bad schools —were the opportunity that so many immigrant groups used to learn the workings and the spirit of American society. In the very worst inner-city schools there are accredited teachers who teach the basics, but too often to students who shun those among them who do well, who see studying as a sucker's game and school itself as a waste of time. One sees in many of these children almost a determination not to learn, a suppression of the natural impulse to understand, which cannot be entirely explained by the determinism of poverty. Out of school, in the neighborhood, these same children learn everything. I think it is the meeting with the mainstream that school symbolizes that clicks them off. In the cultural ethos from which they come, it is always these meetings that trigger the aversion to opportunity, behind which lies inferiority anxiety. Their parents and their culture send them a double message: go to school but don't really apply yourself. The risk is too high.

This same pattern of avoidance, this unconscious circumvention of possibility, is also evident in our commitment to effort—the catalyst of opportunity. Difficult, sustained effort—in school, career, or family life—will be riddled with setbacks, losses, and frustrations. Racial vulnerability erodes effort for blacks by exaggerating the importance of these setbacks, by recasting them as confirmation of racial inferiority rather than the normal pitfalls of sustained effort. The racist anti-self greets these normal difficulties with an I-told-you-so attitude, and the believing self, unwilling to risk seeing that the anti-self is right, may grow timid and pull back from the effort. As with opportunity, racial vulnerability makes hard effort in the mainstream a high-risk activity for blacks.

But this is not the case in those areas where blacks have traditionally excelled. In sports and music, for example, the threat of integration shock is effectively removed. Because so many blacks have succeeded in these areas, a black can enter them without being racially vulnerable. Failure carries no implication of racial inferiority, so the activity itself is far less risky than those in which blacks have no record of special achievement. Certainly, in sports and music one sees blacks sustain the most creative and disciplined effort and then seize opportunities where one would have thought there were none. But all of this changes the instant racial vulnerability becomes a factor. Across the country thousands of young black males take every opportunity and make every effort to reach the elite ranks of the NBA or NFL. But in the classroom, where racial vulnerability is a hidden terror, they and many of their classmates put forth the meagerest effort and show a virtual indifference to the genuine opportunity that is education.

But the most visible circumvention that results from integration shock is the tendency toward self-segregation that, if anything, seems to have increased over the last twenty years. Along with opportunity and effort, it is also white people themselves who are often avoided. I hear young black professionals say they do not socialize with whites after work unless at some "command performance" that comes with the territory of their career. On largely white university campuses where integration shock is particularly intense, black students often try to enforce a kind of neo-separatism that includes black "theme" dorms, black student unions, Afro-houses, black cultural centers, black student lounges, and so on. There is a geopolitics involved in this activity, where race is tied to territory in a way that mimics the whites only/colored only designations of the past. Only now these race spaces are staked out in the name of pride.

I think this impulse to self-segregate, to avoid whites, has to do with the way white people are received by the black anti-self. Even if the believing self wants to see racial difference as essentially meaningless, the anti-self, that hidden perpetrator of racist doubt, sees white people as better than black people. Its mission is to confirm black inferiority, and so it looks closely at whites, watches the way they walk, talk, and negotiate the world, and then grants these styles of being and acting superiority. Somewhere inside every black is a certain awe at the power and achievement of the white race. In every barbershop gripe session where whites are put through the grinder of black anger, there will be a kind of backhanded respect—"Well, he might be evil, but that white boy is smart." True or not, the anti-self organizes its campaign against the believing self's faith in black equality around this supposition. And so, for blacks (as is true for whites in another way), white people in the generic sense have no neutrality. In themselves, they are stimulants to the black anti-self, deliverers of doubt. Their color slips around the deepest need of blacks to believe in their own immutable equality and communes directly with their self-suspicion.

So it is not surprising to hear black students on largely white campuses say that they are simply more comfortable with other blacks. Nor is it surprising to see them caught up in absurd contradictions—demanding separate facilities for themselves even as they protest apartheid in South Africa. Racial vulnerability is a species of fear and, as such, it is the progenitor of countless ironies. More freedom makes us more vulnerable so that in the midst of freedom we feel the impulse to carve our segregated comfort zones that protect us more from our own doubt than from whites. We balk before opportunity and pull back from effort just as these things would bear fruit. We reconstitute the boundaries of segregation just as they become illegal. By averting opportunity and curbing effort for fear of awakening a sense of inferiority, we make inevitable the very failure that shows us inferior.

One of the worst aspects of oppression is that it never ends when the oppressor begins to repent. There is a legacy of doubt in the oppressed that follows long after the cleanest repentance by the oppressor, just as guilt trails the oppressor and makes his redemption incomplete. These themes of doubt and guilt fill in like fresh replacements and work to duplicate the oppression. I think black Americans are today more oppressed by doubt than by racism and that the second phase of our struggle for freedom must be a confrontation with that doubt. Unexamined, this doubt leads us back into the tunnel of our oppression where we reenact our victimization just as society struggles to end its victimization of us. We are not a people formed in freedom. Freedom is always a call to possibility that demands an overcoming of doubt. We are still new to freedom, new to its challenges, new even to the notion that self-doubt can be the slyest enemy of freedom. For us freedom has so long meant the absence of oppression that we have not yet realized it also means the conquering of doubt.

Of course, this does not mean that doubt should become a lake we swim in, but it does mean that we should begin our campaign against doubt by acknowledging it, by outlining the contours of the black anti-self so that we can know and accept exactly what it is that we are afraid of. This is knowledge that can be worked with, knowledge that can point with great precision to the actions through which we can best mitigate doubt and advance ourselves. This is the sort of knowledge that gives the believing self a degree of immunity against the anti-self and that enables it to pile up little victories that, in sum, grant even more immunity.

Certainly inferiority has long been the main theme of the black anti-self, its most lethal weapon against our capacity for self-belief. And so, in a general way, the acceptance of this piece of knowledge implies a mission: to show *ourselves* and (only indirectly) the larger society that we are not inferior in any dimension. That this should already be assumed goes without saying. But what "should be" falls within the province of the believing self, where it has no solidity until the doubt of the anti-self is called out and shown false by demonstrable action in the real world. This is the proof that grants the "should" its rightful solidity, that transforms it from a well-intentioned claim into a certainty.

The temptation is to avoid so severe a challenge, to maintain a black identity, painted in the colors of pride and culture, that provides us with a way of seeing ourselves apart from this challenge. It is easier to be "African-American" than to organize oneself on one's own terms and around one's own aspirations and then, through sustained effort and difficult achievement, put one's insidious anti-self quietly to rest. No black identity, however beautifully conjured, will spare blacks this challenge that, despite its fairness or unfairness, is simply in the nature of things. But then I have faith that in time we will meet this challenge since this, too, is in the nature of things.

4

The Recomposed Self

More on Vulnerability

Racial vulnerability is best thought of not so much as the wound of our oppression as the woundedness we still carry as a result of it—our continuing openness to inferiority anxiety and to racial diminishment and shame. This woundedness is not an inert pain; it is an active agent within the personality that pressures blacks individually and collectively to see ourselves and the world in ways that protect us from our pain and doubt. In this way, racial vulnerability acts as a cause that generates many effects—effects that shape black life in everything from politics to clothing styles, from the way we dance to the way we vote.

What makes racial vulnerability a far worse problem than it need be is the fact that we almost always reflexively deny it. Acknowledging an openness to racial diminishment feels diminishing in itself. The denial impulse kicks in when the believing self is terrorized of being deflated by some whisper of doubt from the anti-self. Denial is a defense against deflation, but its effect is to hide this painful vulnerability so that it can cause countless problems without ever being noticed.

When I was fourteen the mother of a white teammate on the YMCA swimming team would—in a nice but insistent way—correct my grammar when I lapsed into the black English I'd grown up speaking in the neighborhood. She would require that my verbs and pronouns agree, that I put the "g" on my "ings," and that I say "that" instead of "dat." She absolutely abhorred double negatives, and her face would screw up in pain at the sound of one. But her corrections also tapped my racial vulnerability. I felt racial shame at this white woman's fastidious concern with my language. It was as though she was saying that the black part of me was not good enough, would not do, and this is where my denial went to work.

I never admitted to the racial shame I felt. Instead, I decided that she was being racist and humiliating me out of some perverse need to feel better about herself at my expense. And this is the real problem with denial. To deny one reality—my feelings of racial shame—we always create another "reality" to cover over the real one. So there are always two very dangerous elements in any denial—recomposition and distortion. We recompose new feelings to cover over those that threaten us, and these new feelings always distort the threatening situation into something different than what it really is. Rather than feel racial shame, I recomposed this situation into a tableau of racial victimization in which this woman openly scorned my race.

This recomposition gave me some peace for a time because it allowed me to externalize my shame, to transform it into anger at her. But of course, my vulnerability was still at work, and one day when her eyes rolled at some rather glaring lapse, I decided it was time to do something. I told her son I thought she didn't like black people and was taking it out on me. A few days later she marched into the YMCA rec room, took me away from a Ping-Pong game, and sat me down in a corner. It was the late fifties, when certain women painted their faces as though they were canvases, and onto this woman's face were painted a pair of violently red Valentine lips, two perfectly arched eyebrows, and a black beauty mark beside her mouth. It was the distraction of this mask, my wonderment at it, that allowed me to keep my equilibrium.

She told me about herself, that she had grown up poor, had never finished high school, and would never be more than a secretary. She said she didn't give a "good goddamn" about my race, but that if I wanted to do more than "sweat my life away in a steel mill," I better learn to speak correctly. As she continued to talk I was shocked to realize that my comment had genuinely hurt her and that her motive in correcting my English had been no more than simple human kindness. If she had been black, I might have seen this more easily. But she was white, and this fact alone set off a very specific response pattern in which vulnerability to racial shame was the trigger, denial and recomposition the reaction, and a distorted view of the situation the result. This was the sequence by which I converted kindness into harassment and my racial shame into her racism.

I believe this sequence is one of the most unrecognized yet potent forces in contemporary black life. This is the sequence—from racial vulnerability to distortion—that contaminates the perceptual terrain between blacks and whites, between blacks and the American mainstream. Certainly, there are many external forces—economic conditions, cultural patterns, actual racial discrimination, and so on—that affect the way blacks see themselves in the world. But it is racial vulnerability that determines, to a large extent, how we see these forces, what we make of them, and how we act on what we perceive. It is a secret theme of our subjective life, and it is powerful because its influence is both pervasive and invisible.

Integration shock (those shocks of racial doubt that come to blacks in integrated situations) became a greater problem for blacks after the civil rights victories of the early sixties won us new freedoms. Greater freedom meant greater exposure to both our doubt and the denial by which we protected ourselves from it. Segregation, in a sense, saved us from too much denial by limiting our exposure on equal terms to whites. In today's more open society I think we have relied more on denial to escape the racial vulnerability that segregation once buffered us from.

As a result of more denial, we have done more recomposing of our situation since the mid-sixties. In other words, we have tended more to transform our doubts and threats into something different than what they really are and to externalize them by seeing others as responsible for them. I believe there are certain clear themes along which blacks have recomposed denied racial vulnerability. These *themes of recomposition* have always been a part of black life, but in our increased exposure to racial doubt, they have become more vivid and intense than ever before. With the woman who corrected my grammar, I used the theme of victimization to recompose my shame into her racism—I didn't feel shame; I was being victimized. Now the problem was racism rather than shame and she was responsible for it.

Every theme of recomposition has more than a little historical truth. In the case of victimization, for example, there is no doubt that blacks have been, and in some cases still are, victimized because of their race. But when recomposition is at work, this familiar theme of black life is exaggerated and used inappropriately so that distortion always results. When I talk to the current generation of black college students, the sense of victimization is often stronger than any I felt in a segregated grade school in the fifties. I think the sense of being victimized recomposes the denied racial doubt they often feel on largely white college campuses where academic competition is very stiff. So, yes, historically blacks have been terribly victimized, but when today's black college students—who often enjoy preferential admission and many other special concessions—claim victimization, I think that it too often amounts to a recomposition of denied doubts and anxieties they are unwilling to look at.

I am convinced that the distortions our themes of recomposition leave us with are as serious a problem as any we face today as blacks. Fears can never be addressed and overcome when they are redefined as something else and then externalized. For the first time in our history, we do not seem to have a clear sense of our real challenges. Only a knowledge of our vulnerabilities can give us this, and only the continued recomposing of them can hide this knowledge from us.

What makes our themes of recomposition so seductive is that they never look like cover-ups; they look like facts of life. And, in part, they are facts of life, but they are thin, ambiguous facts pushed into a certainty they do not really have, and are used to deny the intolerable vulnerability. They are really themes by which we mythologize ourselves into the appearance of living beyond the reach of racial doubt.

One of the oldest themes of recomposition in black life

might be called compensatory grandiosity. It has been with us for so long because we have needed it to compensate for the diminishment that America so relentlessly made us feel. There are images of it everywhere in black life—the swaggering teenager with his gold chains and suitcase-size ghetto blaster; the "sister" with an insouciant don't-play-with-me attitude; the black college professor with conspicuously perfect elocution and a Latinate vocabulary; the black dock worker who polishes his fingernails; the inflated grandeur of some black preachers; the above-it-all attitude of "cool" that makes the pretense of emotional distance a virtue; the magnificent egotism of a Muhammad Ali. This sort of grandiosity has been an unending source of cultural richness in American life, a gift to all Americans of music and styles of motion. And yet, in many ways, it was born of the need to assert beauty and grace over degradation, to be beautifully human against the charge of inhumanity. It was compensatory.

But compensatory or not, grandiosity has left an indelible mark on black culture and American life in general. It represents the self-insistent spirit of an oppressed people and is a testament to their heart. Yet, as a theme of recomposition, it also has an underside. It can become too much of an escape from diminishment, too much a self-delusion. It can become a form of dependency, a posture of personal or racial specialness that we rely on to keep the demons of doubt at bay. In this lower form, beauty and grace change into self-advertisement, a stance of superiority that we take on for promotional purposes. I think the stresses of integration shock, which have greatly increased in the sixties and seventies and eighties, have made us more dependent on grandiosity as a way to recompose our expanded racial doubt.

When we use grandiosity as a theme of recomposition in

a racial sense, we imply that one area of visible achievement or superiority is only the tip of the iceberg, and that it stands as proof of a broader, underlying superiority. Through this single area we advertise a pervasive superiority that, among other things, compensates for inner fears of inferiority. Beyond compensation, there is also a strong competitive element to grandiosity, since we claim our area of superiority to be more important than the superior areas of other races.

An example of this, I believe, can be seen in what black people call soul. This mysterious spiritual connection to deep human feelings and rhythms is clearly a strong point in black American life (though it is not exclusive to black life). No one can listen to gospel, jazz, blues, or even contemporary music without appreciating this remarkable quality of black life. Yet sometimes our denied racial vulnerability can cause us to overrate this strength, to bask too much in its reflected glory. In other words, we can sometimes use our strength in this area to claim a more pervasive superiority that recomposes the inferiority anxiety we have denied into a grandiose racial specialness that serves our denial. But it may not stop at denial. We may also enter this specialness into competition with the specialness of other races by saying that our *soul* is a far more important area of superiority than those of other races. When we use grandiosity to recompose, we not only achieve denial but also a victory over others that sweetens the denial.

At the large integrated high school I attended (which was 60 percent white), one of the worst sins a black student could be guilty of was not dancing well. Dancing was a manifestation of soul and cool and, as such, it was, among many other things, an advertisement for the race, a visible superiority through which we could recompose at least some of the hidden anxieties of being in an integrated situation. Since most of us came from segregated grade schools, we were enduring a good bit of integration shock, yet on the dance floor our superiority was manifest. At school dances, whites often stopped to look at us in amazement, and we let our strength in this area soothe the anxiety that other areas of school life brought us. This was compensatory grandiosity precisely because we used this single area of superiority to suggest a broader underlying superiority and to win the competition we felt ourselves involved in with whites. If whites were in higher math classes than us, we still had soul, and soul was a vastly more important quality to have as a human being than math ability.

This is how grandiosity works as a theme of recomposition. Without realizing it we had used dancing (and probably athletics too) to create a grandiose mythology about ourselves that may have recomposed our denied vulnerability, but that also led us to compete with whites in an area that had very little to do with success in the American mainstream. But we could not see this. Denial and recomposition always deliver illusion and distortion. If somehow our racial vulnerability had been pointed out to us as a specific form of fear, I think we would have had a perfectly accurate (though challenging) picture of our situation. We were vulnerable in this integrated school to an inferiority anxiety that revolved around its educational purpose. And the only way to ease that anxiety was through academic achievement on a par with other students. No superiority in dancing or sports could alter this fact— which is not to say that these are not valid areas of achievement. It was only our over-reliance on them that obscured our larger challenge.

I think this same theme of recomposition caused some of

the excesses of the late sixties black power movement, several of which are still with us today. Certainly, black nationalism in various forms has always been a force in black American life. But in the mid- and late sixties it virtually exploded onto the American scene and touched every aspect of black life. There were probably many reasons for this, but I think one of them was the sudden exposure to greater freedom that came to us as a result of the civil rights victories in the early sixties. As a people not formed in freedom, whatever vulnerabilities we had were bound to be triggered by the challenges of new freedom. On one level black power, I believe, was a defense against the shock of vulnerability that came automatically with greater freedom.

Blackness itself was transformed into a grandiose quality that suggested a pervasive superiority and allowed us to win the competition with white "superiority." This was done indirectly through suggestion and connotation. Not only was black beautiful, but it was also humane, soulful, earthy, and spiritual. By contrast to whiteness it was not materialistic, militaristic, or mercenary. The black community was grounded in communal love instead of the austere profit motive. We were a natural people in tune with natural forces while whites, out of some spiritual sickness, needed to dominate and control others. White was the color of alienation and black the color of harmony and moral truth.

This was the sort of grandiose mythologizing that allowed us to recompose the shock of vulnerability we experienced in the mid-sixties. For the first time in our history we could no longer merely claim to be equal; new freedoms and opportunities meant that we now had to prove it. But a grandiose blackness recomposed this intimidating challenge by suggesting that we were already proven, in fact superior in those qualities that make a human being human. But recompositions only soothed our doubts with distortion. They never eliminate the real source of our doubt. So, today, we are still left with the same challenge that greater freedom presented us with twenty-five years ago—to achieve parity with other groups in American society. This is not an easy challenge, but neither is it an impossible one.

I don't think black nationalism will help us much in this challenge because it is too infused with defensive grandiosity, too given to bombast and posturing. It is more a hedge against reality than an embrace of it. And wherever one hears its themes today—whether from Louis Farrakhan, black student union leaders, or people in the street—it has that unmistakable ring of compensation, of an illusory black specialness that offers haven from inner doubt. So, even when nationalists espouse black "self-help," this admirable message is undermined by a grandiosity that makes self-interested action unnecessary. One can be a black nationalist without having to do very much, without going as far in school as one can possibly go, without opening a business and making it thrive, without testing one's dreams against the grit of reality. People who do these things are rarely nationalists themselves, though they might fellow-travel a little in a nod to black unity. We are only predisposed to the glamour of black nationalism when the reservoir of self-doubt is deep and the need to recompose powerful.

Probably the most common theme of recomposition is the claim of racial victimization. It is a particularly dangerous recomposition because it is so obviously grounded in historical fact. No one can deny that blacks were horribly victimized in the past, and no one can say with certainty that subtle forms of this victimization don't continue today. Certainly, poverty itself, which is far too common among blacks, is often equated with victimization whether or not those who endure it today do so because they have been racially victimized. Victimization is a broad, somewhat sloppy word that one can apply to oneself in the most subjective of ways. And when we do think of ourselves as victims, we are released from responsibility for some difficulty, spared some guilt and accountability. Our innocence is restored because an injustice was done to us. Injustice is what gives the claim of victimization its magic, its power to spray the onus of responsibility on others.

By any human standard, black Americans have endured a terrible injustice. And so, when blacks take the floor and point to their difficulties as evidence of victimization, refutation is not easy—it feels like a continuation of the act of victimizing, like blaming the victim. After victimization has been acknowledged, as it has been in the case of blacks, it takes on an enormous authority and power. Thus, quite apart from the reality of actual victimization, it becomes very seductive as a theme of recomposition. In integrated situations, where blacks may experience much racial vulnerability but little or no actual victimization, there will be a temptation to recompose that vulnerability into victimization because our historic role as victims gives our claim such authority.

In the last twenty-five years the stresses of new freedom, which have greatly intensified black vulnerability, have led us, I believe, to claim more racial victimization than we have actually endured, as a way of recomposing that unacknowledged vulnerability. Again, this is not to say that we have not experienced victimization, only that our claims have been excessive. Evidence of this can be seen in the one-sided approach that the civil rights establishment has taken toward black problems. Though we have gained equality under law and even special entitlements through social programs and affirmative action, our leadership continues to stress our victimization. On the basis of this emphasis they have demanded concessions from government, industry, and society at large while demanding very little from blacks themselves by way of living up to the opportunities that have already been won. Our leaders still see us as victims, as people who can only be helped from the outside. When black male college enrollment began to decline in the eighties, they said it was because President Reagan cut student loan programs, a rather absurd claim of victimization when we consider that black female enrollment increased slightly during this period. Certainly, our civil rights leaders should do everything to remedy any racial victimization that remains in society, but their singular focus in this area only encourages us to use victimization to recompose our anxieties.

Because black leadership has, itself, recomposed the doubts of its own people, it has settled on a very distorted view of their situation. By seeing only victimization, they missed the fact that in 1964, when the Civil Rights Bill was passed, we were a people with very little experience of real freedom. As many have said, this bill was more an Emancipation Proclamation than the earlier one. But, though it delivered greater freedom, it did not deliver the skills and attitudes that are required to thrive in freedom. Freedom is stressful, difficult, and frightening—a "burden," according to Sartre, because of the responsibility it carries. Oppression conditions people *away* from all the values and attitudes one needs in freedom—individual initiative, self-interested hard work, individual responsibility, delayed gratification, and so on. In oppression these things don't pay off and are therefore negatively reinforced. It is not that these values have never had a presence in black life, only that they were muted and destabilized by the negative conditioning of oppression. I believe that since the mid-sixties our weakness in this area has been a far greater detriment to our advancement than any remaining racial victimization.

It is rarely wise to compare blacks to other minority groups, but in this context it may be helpful. Asians from various backgrounds—particularly recent immigrants from Southeast Asia—have certainly endured racial discrimination and hostility. Yet, as a group, they have by most measures thrived in America. One of the things this indicates is that, today, race is not the determining variable it once was. I think the difference between black and Asian success turns on the fact that Asians came to this country with values well suited to the challenges and opportunities of freedom. I make this comparison only to underscore the importance of these values, not to inflate Asians or condemn blacks. Nevertheless, our leadership, and black Americans in general, have woefully neglected the power and importance of these values. Still, we must not be too hard on ourselves. New to freedom, it was hard to know the vulnerabilities it would trigger. Our victimization was so painfully obvious—and never more so than in the fresh light of new freedom—that it was hard to know that we had inner doubt, and harder even still to understand that we were recomposing that doubt into a distorted view of our situation, a re-embrace of what we had just virtually overcome. I don't think we will have a true black leadership until there is a willingness to break through the

distortion that sees victimization as the primary black problem. We need a leadership that names our doubts and then
insists on the values by which we can defeat them.

The most difficult theme of recomposition to be aware of,
I believe, is the black American identity itself, or at least
the particular form of that identity with us today. The racial
element of our overall identity recomposes racial doubt by
suppressing the aspect of our identity that is uniquely individual. Our individuality may lead us into situations that
threaten us racially, and when this happens the racial part
of the identity may step in and recompose the situation in a
way that spares us the vulnerability, but also represses the
individuality that exposed us to it in the first place. An extreme example of this is the black student who once told me
that he was not sure he should master standard English because then he "wouldn't be black no more." The individual
part of his identity could see the need to improve his English,
but this need also exposed him to racial vulnerability—the
inferiority anxiety he would surely feel as a college student
still mastering basic English. To avoid this vulnerability he
claimed that his need to identify with black people—to
proudly speak their form of English—made learning standard
English a questionable enterprise. His racial identity recomposed his individual desire because that desire exposed him
to vulnerability. For this young man, race was the ultimate
arbiter of his individuality not because, I believe, he was so
loyal to his race, but because race excused his fears. Racial
identity is a necessary element in the overall identity of any
black, but when we *use* it to recompose our fears, we always
suppress our individuality and create a distorted view of ourselves and the world.

What we're really doing here is using racial identity—our

natural need to feel a part of our people—as a censor against our own individuality. As individuals, blacks cannot help but want the same sorts of things all individuals want, namely, a better life—an education, a home, a prosperous career, a well-cared-for family, maybe fame and wealth. But the pursuit of these things will inevitably draw us into the American mainstream where we will surely encounter much racial vulnerability. And this is the point at which our racial identity, out of the impulse to make us seem proud and invulnerable, can become a hegemonic censor that holds us back by recomposing vulnerability in such a way that moving ahead as an individual amounts to racial betrayal. This process is evident in one of the most damning things one black can say about another black—"So-and-so is not really black, so-and-so is an Oreo." The tragedy in this is that, very often, so-and-so is more successful than other blacks and more comfortable as an individual in the mainstream.

Again, I believe it is the great increase in racial vulnerability, a companion of new freedom, that drew the black identity into its role as a censor of black individuality. When a people of a race or nation are insecure about their ability to thrive in the larger world, they inevitably evolve an identity that allows them to recompose inner fears into external threats. It is not that we fear whether we can thrive as well as others; it is that others are hostile to us, and we must be tightly unified to defend ourselves. There is always an element of paranoia in this sort of identity. Individuality is dangerous to such an identity because it threatens to reveal that inner fears are the real problem. When a black is comfortable and successful in the mainstream, he or she shows that the external threat is not as serious as many blacks wish to think and, correspondingly, that inner doubt is a more powerful regressive force. *The most dangerous threat to the black identity is not the racism of white society (this actually confirms the black identity), but the black who insists on his or her own individuality.*

To stop this threat, the black identity censors individuality by enforcing a rigid "party line." To be certified as black, one must take on this party line—in spirit if not in detail— as an internal censor against those individual impulses that would transgress it. Today the pressure to subscribe is particularly intense, I think, because we are more challenged and therefore more racially vulnerable than ever before. Subscription to this identity earns us the right to use it as a haven against this vulnerability. It is no accident that more than 90 percent of blacks have voted Democratic in the last several presidential elections, even when blacks had no chance of gaining political leverage by doing so. Identity over politics is the rule when vulnerability is the unseen enemy.

The party line itself is a loose series of broad assumptions that ultimately lead to specific positions. Some of these assumptions are that white racism and racial discrimination are still the primary black problem; that blacks should maintain an essentially adversarial stance toward the mainstream; that institutional racism is automatically present in the workplace; that political conservatism is by definition anti-black; that blacks are not "given" enough chances to advance; that blacks are exploited economically and otherwise because they are black; that the larger society is basically indifferent to the problems of blacks; that high black crime rates are the outgrowth of victimization; that blacks must work twice as hard to gain recognition as whites; that one should be black first and American second; etc. All of this translates into specific political positions: being pro-Arab and anti-Israeli; being in favor of affirmative action; being against the Republican party and in favor of Jesse Jackson, no matter what office he aspires to; being in favor of representational diversity in education and the workplace, even when it is not supported by an underlying racial parity; etc.

Though there is some truth in many of these assumptions, their overall effect is to make the black identity an identity of accusation that offers its subscribers a way to recompose their vulnerability into their victimization. Nowhere in the current black identity is there a strong theme of responsibility for our own fate, nor are there positive themes that define our character as a people or highlight our many strengths. It is an identity formed in the caldron of racial politics, and its primary assumptions accuse others and defend ourselves.

The defensiveness and rigidity of this identity is nowhere more evident than in its punitive stance toward individual blacks who openly dissent from the party line. For these blacks there is an excommunicative sanction. Recently, at the University of Massachusetts—Amherst, the Afro-American Studies department formally asked the university administration to "reassign" the black writer Julius Lester to a different department because, in his latest book, he had characterized a public comment by James Baldwin as anti-Semitic. But this was not Lester's only "crime." Some years earlier he had, for very personal reasons eloquently detailed in his book *Lovesong: Becoming a Jew*, converted to Judaism. In accord with his new faith, he had, in the late seventies, joined those asking for Andrew Young's resignation as UN Ambassador because of Young's secret meeting with leaders of the PLO. This was too much individuality for the current black identity to handle, especially given Lester's status as a public figure. One black colleague called him an "anti-

Negro Negro," and the chairman of Afro-American Studies is said to have told his dean that, "If you don't get Lester out of the department, we'll make his life miserable." Lester was reassigned to the Department of Judaic and Near Eastern Studies. He was excommunicated.

Julius Lester's individuality transgresses the current black identity precisely because it threatens the network of assumptions by which this identity defends blacks against racial vulnerability. This identity cannot include a man like Lester and still serve its defensive function. If we include him we must also include the range of freedom he is willing to demand for himself, and this, for the time being, is too much. The tragedy in this is made clear in those profound lines from Ralph Ellison's *Invisible Man*: "Our task is that of making ourselves individuals. The conscience of a race is the gift of its individuals."

It is easy to see how Lester was a victim of this intolerant identity, but I think those who sought his removal, as well as blacks generally, are also its victims. This identity not only censors our individuality but also prescribes a rigid racial protocol—internally repressive, externally divisive— by which we censor each other. The effect of this censoring is to disallow authentic critical voices and, therefore, to stifle healthy debate within the black community. The few critical voices we have—Thomas Sowell, William Julius Wilson, Glenn Loury—are too often disregarded rather than debated, despite the fact that renewal and growth do not happen without debate. Again, I believe it is a racial vulnerability that leads us circuitously through denial and recomposition into an identity that sinks us in defensiveness, that makes our own individuality dangerous, and that smothers the open debate we must have in order to know ourselves.

The woman I mentioned at the outset who always corrected my grammar was blithe to the racial doubt that her efforts brought to life in me. And even when that doubt came to light in my recomposed judgment of her as a racist, she was unwilling to be stopped by it. Without denying it, she would not allow it to have any power. After our little talk she continued to monitor my use of the language—now with my cooperation—for as long as I knew her. Of course, what she did for me was a gift. But this gift was only secondarily related to better grammar. The real gift was that she helped me to see how easy it is to delude oneself where race is concerned. When she would not allow me my distortion, I had to see the simplest thing: there was really nothing to be afraid of.

Now, I know that my fear predated this woman. It was a conditional vulnerability, the gift of history. Yet when she took away my distortion she also released me from my vulnerability. And this is how I think it will have to work for black Americans in general. To find release from racial vulnerability we will have to discover what is clearly distorted in our vision of our situation in America—a sort of working backward through the embroidery of fear past the fear itself. For a time we will have to do for ourselves what this woman did for me: monitor our impulse to deny and recompose. For this, we will need all the critical voices we can find. It is only our vulnerability that makes us afraid of such voices. I believe that the next collective challenge for black America is simply to walk out and meet the words and ideas that make us tense.

5

White Guilt

―――――――■―――――――

I don't remember hearing the phrase "white guilt" very much before the mid-sixties. Growing up black in the fifties, I never had the impression that whites were much disturbed by guilt when it came to blacks. When I would stray into the wrong restaurant in pursuit of a hamburger, it didn't occur to me that the waitress was unduly troubled by guilt when she asked me to leave. I can see now that possibly she was, but then all I saw was her irritability at having to carry out so unpleasant a task. If there was guilt, it was mine for having made an imposition of myself. Frankly, I can remember feeling a certain sympathy for such people, as if *I* was victimizing *them* by drawing them out of an innocent anonymity into the unasked-for role of racial policemen. Occasionally, they came right out and asked me to feel sorry for them. A caddy master at a country club told my brother and me that he was doing us a favor by not letting us caddy at this white club, and that we should try to understand his position, "put yourselves in my shoes." Our color had brought this man anguish and, if a part of that anguish was guilt, it was not as immediate to me as my own guilt. I smiled at the man to let him know he shouldn't feel bad and then began the long walk home. Certainly, I also judged him a coward, but in that era his cowardice was something I had to absorb.

In the sixties, particularly the black-is-beautiful late sixties, this sort of absorption was no longer necessary. The lines of moral power, like plates in the earth, had shifted. White guilt became so palpable you could see it on people. At the time, what it looked like to my eyes was a remarkable loss of authority. And what whites lost in authority, blacks gained. You cannot feel guilty toward anyone without giving away power to them. So, suddenly, this huge vulnerability opened up in whites and, as a black, you had the power to step right into it. In fact, black power all but demanded that you do so. What shocked me in the late sixties, after the helplessness I had felt in the fifties, was that guilt had changed the nature of the white man's burden from the administration of inferiors to the uplift of equals, from the obligations of dominance to the urgencies of repentance.

I think what made the difference between the fifties and sixties, as far as white guilt was concerned, was that whites in the sixties underwent an archetypal Fall. Because of the immense turmoil of the civil rights movement, and later the black power movement, whites were confronted for more than a decade with their willingness to participate in or comply with the oppression of blacks, their indifference to human suffering and denigration, their capacity to abide evil for their own benefit, and in defiance of their own sacred principles. The 1964 Civil Rights Act that bestowed equality under the law on blacks was also, in a certain sense, an admission of white guilt. Had white society not been wrong, there would have been no need for such an act. In this act, the nation acknowledged its fallen state, its lack of racial innocence, and confronted the incriminating self-knowledge that it had rationalized flagrant injustice. Denial is a common way of handling guilt, but in the sixties there was little will left for denial except in the most recalcitrant whites. And with this defense lost, there was really only one road back to innocence—through actions and policies that would bring redemption.

I believe that in the sixties the need for white redemption from racial guilt became the most powerful, yet unspoken, element in America's social-policy-making process, first giving rise to the Great Society and then to a series of programs, policies, and laws that sought to make black equality and restitution a national mission. Once America could no longer deny guilt, it went after redemption, or at least the look of redemption, with a vengeance. Yet today, some twenty years later, study after study tells us that, by many measures, the gap between blacks and whites is widening rather than narrowing. A University of Chicago study indicates that segregation is more entrenched in American cities today than ever imagined. A National Research Council study says the "status of blacks relative to whites (in housing and education) has stagnated or regressed since the early seventies." A follow-up to the famous Kerner Commission Report says we are as much at risk today of becoming a "nation within a nation" as we were twenty years ago when the original report was made.

I think the white need for redemption has contributed to this tragic situation by shaping our policies regarding blacks in ways that might deliver the look of innocence to society

and its institutions, but that do very little to actually uplift
blacks. Specifically, the effect of this hidden need has been
to bend social policy more toward reparation for black oppression than toward the much harder and more mundane work
of black uplift and development. Rather than facilitate the
development of blacks to parity with whites, these programs
and policies—affirmative action is a good example—have
tended to give blacks special entitlements that in many cases
are of no use because we lack the development that would
put us in a position to take advantage of them. I think the
reason there has been more entitlement than development is
(along with black power) the unacknowledged white need for
redemption—not true redemption, which would have focused
policy on black development, but the appearance of redemption which requires only that society, in the name of
development, seem to be paying back its former victims with
preferences. One of the effects of entitlements, I believe, has
been to encourage in blacks a dependency both on the entitlements and on the white guilt that generates them. Even
when it serves ideal justice, bounty from another man's guilt
weakens. This is not the only factor in black "stagnation"
and "regression," but I do believe it is one factor.

It is easy enough to say that white guilt too often has the
effect of bending social policies in the wrong direction. But
what exactly is this guilt, and how does it work in American
life?

I think that white guilt, in its broad sense, springs from a
knowledge of ill-gotten advantage. More precisely, it comes
from the juxtaposition of this knowledge with the inevitable
gratitude one feels for being white rather than black in America. Given the moral instincts of human beings, it is all but

impossible to enjoy an ill-gotten advantage, much less to feel at least secretly grateful for it, without consciously or unconsciously experiencing guilt. If, as Kierkegaard says, "innocence is ignorance," then guilt must always involve knowledge. White Americans *know* that their historical advantage comes from the subjugation of an entire people. So, even for whites today for whom racism is anathema, there is no escape from the knowledge that makes for guilt. Racial guilt simply accompanies the condition of being white in America.

I do not believe that this guilt is a crushing anguish for most whites, but I do believe it constitutes an ongoing racial vulnerability, an openness to racial culpability, that is a thread in white life, sometimes felt, sometimes not, but ever present as a potential feeling. In the late sixties almost any black could charge this thread with enough current for a white to feel it. I had a friend who developed this activity into a sort of specialty. I don't think he meant to be mean, though certainly he was mean. I think he was, in that hyperbolic era, exhilarated by the discovery that his race, which had long been a liability, now gave him a certain edge—that white guilt was black power. To feel this power he would sometimes set up what he called "race experiments." Once I watched him stop a white businessman in a large hotel men's room and convince him to increase his tip to the black attendant from one to twenty dollars.

My friend's tact in this was very simple, even corny. Out of the attendant's earshot he asked the man to simply look at the attendant, a frail, elderly, and very dark man in a starched white smock that made the skin on his neck and face look as leathery as a turtle's. He sat listlessly, pathetically, on a straight-backed chair next to a small table on which sat a stack of hand towels and a silver plate for tips. Since he offered no service beyond the handing out of towels, one could only conclude the hotel management offered his lowly presence as flattery to their patrons, as an opportunity for that easy noblesse oblige that could reassure even the harried, wrung-out traveling salesman of his superior station. My friend was quick to make this point to the businessman and to say that no white man would do in this job. But when the businessman put the single back in his wallet and took out a five, my friend only sneered. Did he understand the tragedy of a life spent this way, of what it must be like to earn one's paltry living as a symbol of inferiority? And did he realize that his privilege as an affluent white businessman (ironically, he had just spent the day trying to sell a printing press to the Black Muslims for their newspaper *Muhammad Speaks*) was connected to the deprivation of this man and others like him?

But then my friend made a mistake that ended the game. In the heat of argument, which until then had only been playfully challenging, he inadvertently mentioned his father. This stopped him cold and his eyes turned inward. "What about your father?" the businessman asked. "He had a hard life, that's all." "How did he have a hard life?" Now my friend was on the defensive. I knew he did not get along with his father, a bitter man who worked nights in a factory and demanded that the house be dark and silent all day. My friend blamed his father's bitterness on racism, but I knew he had not meant to exploit his own pain in this silly "experiment." Things had gotten too close to home, but he didn't know how to get out of the situation without losing face. Now, caught in his own trap, he did what he least wanted to do. He gave forth the rage he truly felt to a white stranger in a public men's room. "My father never had a chance," he said with the kind of anger that could easily turn to tears. "He never had a fuckin' chance. Your father had all the goddamn chances, and you know he did. You sell printing presses to black people and make thousands and your father probably lives down in Fat City, Florida, somewhere, all because you're white." On and on he went in this vein, using—against all that was honorable in him—his own profound racial pain to extract a flash of guilt from a white man he didn't even know.

He got more than a flash. The businessman was touched. His eyes became mournful and finally he simply said, "You're right. Your people got a raw deal." He took a twenty-dollar bill from his wallet, then walked over and dropped it in the old man's tip plate. When he was gone my friend and I could not look at the old man, nor could we look at each other.

It is obvious that this was a rather shameful encounter for all concerned—my friend and I as his silent accomplice— trading on our racial pain, tampering with a stranger for no reason, and the stranger then buying his way out of the situation for twenty dollars, a sum that was generous by one count and cheap by another. It was not an encounter of people but of historical grudges and guilts. Yet, when I think about it now, twenty years later, I see that it had all the elements of a paradigm that I believe has been very much at the heart of racial policy-making in America since the sixties.

My friend did two things that made this businessman vulnerable to his guilt, that brought his guilt into the situation as a force. First, he put this man in touch with his own *knowledge* of his ill-gotten advantage as a white. The effect of this was to disallow the man any pretense of racial innocence, to let him know that even if he was not the sort of white who used the word *nigger* around the dinner table, he still had reason to feel racial guilt. But as disarming as this might have been, it was too abstract to do much more than crack open his vulnerability, to expose him to the logic of white guilt. This was the five-dollar intellectual sort of guilt. The twenty dollars required something more visceral. In achieving this, the second thing my friend did was something that he had not intended to do, something that ultimately brought him as much shame as he was passing out. He made a display of his own racial pain and anger. (What brought him shame was not the pain and anger but his trading on them for what turned out to be a mere twenty bucks.) The effect of this display was to reinforce the man's knowledge of ill-gotten advantage, to give credibility and solidity to it by putting a face on it. Here was human testimony, a young black beside himself at the thought of his father's racially constricted life. The pain of one man evidenced the knowledge of the other. When the businessman listened to my friend's pain, his racial guilt—normally one guilt lying dormant among others—was called out like a neglected debt he would finally have to settle. An ill-gotten advantage is not hard to bear—it can be marked up to fate—until it touches the human pain it brought into the world. This is the pain that hardens guilty knowledge.

Such knowledge is a powerful pressure when it becomes conscious. And what makes it so powerful is the element of fear that guilt always carries, fear of what the guilty knowledge says about us. Guilt makes us afraid for ourselves and so generates as much self-preoccupation as concern for others. The nature of this preoccupation is always the redemption of innocence, the reestablishment of good feeling about oneself.

In this sense, the fear for the self that is buried in all guilt is a pressure toward selfishness. It can lead us to put our own need for innocence above our concern for the problem that made us feel guilt in the first place. But this fear for the self not only inspires selfishness; it also becomes a pressure to *escape* the guilt-inducing situation. When selfishness and escapism are at work, we are no longer interested in the source of our guilt and, therefore, no longer concerned with an authentic redemption from it. Now we only want the *look* of redemption, the gesture of concern that will give us the appearance of innocence and escape from the situation. Obviously, the businessman did not put twenty dollars in the tip plate because he thought it would go to the uplift of black Americans. He did it selfishly for the appearance of concern and for the escape it afforded him.

This is not to say that guilt is never the right motive for doing good works or showing concern, only that it is a very dangerous one because of its tendency to draw us into self-preoccupation and escapism. Guilt is a civilizing emotion when the fear for the self it carries is contained—a containment that allows guilt to be more selfless and that makes genuine concern possible. I think this was the kind of guilt that, along with other forces, made the 1964 Civil Rights Act possible. But, since then, I believe too many of our social policies related to race have been shaped by the fearful underside of guilt.

Black power evoked white guilt and made it a force in American institutions, just as my friend brought it to life in the businessman. Not many volunteer for guilt. Usually, it is others that make us feel it. It was the expression of black anger and pain that hardened the guilty knowledge of white ill-gotten advantage. And black power—whether from militant fringe groups, the civil rights establishment, or big city political campaigns—knew exactly the kind of white guilt it was after. It wanted to trigger the kind of white guilt in which whites fear for their own decency and innocence; it wanted the guilt of white self-preoccupation and escapism. Always at the heart of black power, in whatever form, there has been a profound anger at what was done to blacks and an equally profound feeling that there should be reparations. But a sober white guilt in which fear for the self is contained is only good for strict fairness—the 1964 Civil Rights Act that guaranteed equality under the law. It is of little value when one is after more than fairness. So black power made it its mission to have whites fear for their innocence, to feel a visceral guilt from which they would have to seek a more profound redemption. In such redemption was the possibility of black reparation. Black power upped the ante on white guilt.

With black power, all the elements of the hidden paradigm that shapes America's race-related social policy were in place. Knowledge of ill-gotten advantage could now be evidenced and deepened by black power into the sort of guilt from which institutions could redeem themselves only by offering more than fairness—by offering forms of reparation and compensation for past injustice. I believe this was the paradigm that bent our policies toward racial entitlements at the expense of racial development. In 1964, one of the assurances that Senator Hubert Humphrey and other politicians had to give Congress in order to get the landmark Civil Rights Bill passed was that the bill would not in any way require employers to use racial preferences to rectify racial imbalances. But this was before the explosion of black power in the late sixties, before the hidden paradigm was set in motion. After black power, racial preferences became the order of the day.

If this paradigm brought blacks entitlements, it also

brought us the continuation of our most profound problem in American society: our invisibility as a people. The white guilt that this paradigm elicits is the kind of guilt that preoccupies whites with their own innocence and pressures them toward escapism—twenty dollars in the plate and out the door. With this guilt, as opposed to the contained guilt of genuine concern, whites tend to see only their own need for quick redemption. Blacks, then, become a means to this redemption and, as such, they must be seen as generally "less than" others. Their needs are "special," "unique," "different." They are seen exclusively along the dimension of their victimization, so they become "different" people with whom whites can negotiate entitlements, but never fully see as people like themselves. Guilt that preoccupies people with their own innocence blinds them to those who make them feel guilty. This, of course, is not racism, and yet it has the same effect as racism since it makes blacks something of a separate species for whom normal standards and values do not automatically apply.

Nowhere is this more evident today than in American universities. At some of America's most elite universities, administrators have granted concessions in response to black student demands (black power) that all but sanction racial separatism on campus—black "theme" dorms, black students unions, black yearbooks, homecoming dances, and so on. I don't believe administrators sincerely believe in these separatist concessions. Most of them are liberals who see racial separatism as wrong. But black student demands pull them into the paradigm of self-preoccupied white guilt whereby they seek a quick redemption by offering special entitlements that go beyond fairness. In this black students become invisible to them. Though blacks have the lowest grade point average of any group in American universities, administrators never sit down with them and "demand" in kind that they bring their grades up to par. The paradigm of white guilt makes the real problems of black students secondary to the need for white redemption. It also cuts these administrators off from their own values, which would most certainly discourage racial separatism and encourage higher black performance. Lastly, it makes for escapist policies; there is little difference between giving black students a separate graduation ceremony or student lounge and leaving twenty dollars in the tip plate on the way out the door.

What demonstrates more than anything the degree to which university administrators (and faculties) have been subdued by this paradigm is their refusal to lead black students, to tell them what they honestly think, to insist that they perform at a higher level, and to ask them to integrate themselves fully into campus life. This marks the difference between self-preoccupied guilt and the guilt of genuine concern, where fear for one's innocence is contained. The former grants entitlements as a means to easy innocence and escape from judgment; the latter refuses the entanglements and blindness of self-concerned guilt and, out of honest concern, demands black development.

Escapist racial policies—policies whereby institutions favor black entitlement over development out of a preoccupation with their own innocence—have, I believe, a dispiriting impact on blacks. Such policies have the effect of transforming whites from victimizers into patrons and keeping blacks where they have always been—dependent on the largesse of whites. This was made evident in a famous statement by President Lyndon Johnson at Howard University in 1965: "You do not take a person who, for years, has been hobbled by chains and liberate him, bring him up to the starting line of a race and then say, 'You're free to compete with others,' and justly believe that you have been fair."

On its surface this seems to be the most reasonable of statements, but on closer examination we can see how it deflects the emphasis away from black responsibility and toward white responsibility. The actors in this statement— "You [whites] do not *take* a person [blacks] . . ."—are whites; blacks are the passive recipients of white action. The former victimizers are challenged now to be patrons, but where is the black challenge? This is really a statement to and about white people, their guilt, their responsibility, and their road to redemption. Not only does it not enunciate a black mission, but it sees blacks only in the dimension of their victimization—"hobbled by chains"—and casts them once again in the role of receivers of white beneficence. Nowhere in this utterance does President Johnson show respect for black resilience, or faith in the capacity of blacks to run fast once they get to the "starting line." This statement, which launched Johnson's Great Society, had the two ever-present signposts of white guilt—white self-preoccupation and black invisibility.

White guilt has pressured many of America's racial policies toward a paternalism that makes it difficult for blacks to find their true mettle or develop a faith in their own capacity to run as fast as others. The most vivid examples of this are the many forms of preferential treatment that come under the heading of affirmative action—an escapist racial policy, I believe, that offers entitlements, rather than development, to blacks. A preference is not a training program; it teaches no skills, instills no values. It only makes a color a passport.

But the worst aspect of racial preferences is that they encourage dependency on entitlements rather than on our own initiative, a situation that has already led many blacks to believe that we cannot have fairness without entitlements. And here we fall into an Orwellian double-speak where preference means equality. At the heart of this confusion, I believe, is an unspoken black doubt about our ability to compete that is covered over by a preoccupation with racial discrimination. Since there are laws to protect us against discrimination, preferences only impute a certain helplessness to blacks that diminishes our self-esteem. The self-preoccupied form of white guilt that is behind racial preferences always makes us lower so that we can be lifted up.

Recently, Penn State launched a program that actually pays black students for improving their grades—a C to C + average brings $550, and anything more brings $1,100. Here is the sort of guilty kindness that kills. What kind of self-respect is a black student going to have as he or she reaches out to take $550 for C work when many white students would be embarrassed by so average a performance? What better way to drive home the nail of inferiority? And what more Pavlovian system of conditioning blacks to dependency than shelling out cash for grades? Here, black students learn to hustle their victimization rather than overcome it while their patrons escape with the cheapest sort of innocence. Not all preferential treatment is this insidious, but the same dynamic is always at work when color brings entitlement.

I think effective racial policies can only come from the sort of white guilt where fear for the self is contained so that genuine concern can emerge. The test for this healthy guilt is simply a heartfelt feeling of concern without any compromise of one's highest values and principles. But how can whites reach this more selfless form of guilt? I believe the only way is to slacken one's grip on innocence. Guilt has always been the lazy man's way to innocence—I feel guilt *because* I am innocent, guilt confirms my innocence. It is the compulsion to always think of ourselves as innocent that binds us to self-preoccupied guilt. Whites in general, and particularly those public and private institutions (not necessarily white) that make racial policy, must not be so preoccupied with their image of innocence or, put another way, their public relations of good intentions. What is needed now is a new spirit of pragmatism in racial matters where blacks are seen simply as American citizens who deserve complete fairness and in some cases developmental assistance, but in no case special entitlements based on color. We need deracinated social policies that attack poverty rather than *black* poverty and that instill those values that make for self-reliance. The white message to blacks must be: America hurt you badly and that is wrong, but entitlements only prolong the hurt while development overcomes it.

Selfish white guilt is really self-importance. It has no humility and it asks for an unreasonable, egotistical innocence. Nothing diminishes a black more than this sort of guilt in a white, which to my mind amounts to a sort of moral colonialism. We used to say in the sixties that at least in the South you knew where you stood. I always thought this was a little foolish since I didn't like where I stood there. But I think one of the things we meant by this—at the time—was that the South had little investment in its racial innocence and that this was very liberating in an ironical sort of way.

It meant there would be no undercurrent of enmeshment with white need. It gave us back ourselves. The selfishly guilty white is drawn to what blacks least like in themselves—their suffering, victimization, and dependency. This is no good for anyone.

6

On Being Black and Middle Class

Not long ago, a friend of mine, black like myself, said to me that the term *black middle class* was actually a contradiction in terms. Race, he insisted, blurred class distinctions among blacks. If you were black, you were just black and that was that. When I argued, he let his eyes roll at my naïveté. Then he went on. For us, as black professionals, it was an exercise in self-flattery, a pathetic pretension, to give meaning to such a distraction. Worse, the very idea of class threatened the unity that was vital to the black community as a whole. After all, since when had white America taken note of anything but color when it came to blacks? He then reminded me of an old Malcolm X line that had been popular in the sixties. Question: What is a black man with a Ph.D.? Answer: A nigger.

For many years I had been on my friend's side of this argument. Much of my conscious thinking on the old conundrum of race and class was shaped during my high school and college years in the race-charged sixties, when the fact of my race took on an almost religious significance. Progressively, from the mid-sixties on, more and more aspects of my life found their explanation, their justification, and their motivation in my race. My youthful concerns about career, romance, money, values, and even styles of dress became subject to consultation with various oracular sources of racial wisdom. And these ranged from a figure as ennobling as Martin Luther King, Jr., to the underworld elegance of dress I found in jazz clubs on the South Side of Chicago. Everywhere there were signals, and in those days I considered myself so blessed with clarity and direction that I pitied my white classmates who found more embarrassment than guidance in the fact of *their* race. In 1968, inflated by new power, I took a mischievous delight in calling them culturally disadvantaged.

But now, hearing my friend's comment was like hearing a priest from a church I'd grown disenchanted with. I understood him, but my faith was weak. What had sustained me in the sixties sounded monotonous and off-the-mark in the eighties. For me, race had lost much of its juju, its singular capacity to conjure meaning. And today, when I honestly look at my life and the lives of many other middle-class blacks I know, I can see that race never fully explained our situation in American society. Black though I may be, it is impossible for me to sit in my single-family house with two cars in the driveway and a swing set in the backyard and *not* see the role class has played in my life. And how can my friend, similarly raised and similarly situated, not see it?

Yet despite my certainty I felt a sharp tug of guilt as I tried to explain myself over my friend's skepticism. He is a man of many comedic facial expressions and, as I spoke, his brow lifted in extreme moral alarm as if I were uttering the unspeakable. His clear implication was that I was being elitist and possibly (dare we suggest?) anti-black—crimes for which there might well be no redemption. He pretended to fear for me. I chuckled along with him, but inwardly I did wonder at myself. Though I never doubted the validity of what I was saying, I felt guilty saying it. Why?

After he left (to retrieve his daughter from a dance lesson) I realized that the trap I felt myself in had a tiresome familiarity and, in a sort of slow motion epiphany, I began to see its outline. It was like the suddenly sharp vision one has at the end of a burdensome marriage when all the long-repressed incompatibilities come undeniably to light.

What became clear to me is that people like myself, my friend, and middle-class blacks in general are caught in a very specific double bind that keeps two equally powerful elements of our identity at odds with each other. The middle-class values by which we were raised—the work ethic, the importance of education, the value of property ownership, of respectability, of "getting ahead," of stable family life, of initiative, of self-reliance, et cetera—are, in themselves, raceless and even assimilationist. They urge us toward participation in the American mainstream, toward integration, toward a strong identification with the society, and toward the entire constellation of qualities that are implied in the word individualism. These values are almost rules for how to prosper in a democratic, free enterprise society that admires and rewards individual effort. They tell us to work hard for ourselves and our families and to seek our opportunities whenever they appear, inside or outside the confines of whatever ethnic group we may belong to.

But the particular pattern of racial identification that

emerged in the sixties and that still prevails today urges middle-class blacks (and all blacks) in the opposite direction. This pattern asks us to see ourselves as an embattled minority, and it urges an adversarial stance toward the mainstream and an emphasis on ethnic consciousness over individualism. It is organized around an implied separatism.

The opposing thrust of these two parts of our identity results in the double bind of middle-class blacks. There is no forward movement on either plane that does not constitute backward movement on the other. This was the familiar trap I felt myself in while talking with my friend. As I spoke about class, his eyes reminded me that I was betraying race. Clearly, the two indispensable parts of my identity were a threat to one another.

Of course when you think about it, class and race are both similar in some ways and also naturally opposed. They are two forms of collective identity with boundaries that intersect. But whether they clash or peacefully coexist has much to do with how they are defined. Being both black and middle-class becomes a double bind when class and race are defined in sharply antagonistic terms, so that one must be repressed to appease the other.

But what is the "substance" of these two identities, and how does each establish itself in an individual's overall identity?

It seems to me that when we identify with any collective we are basically identifying with images that tell us what it means to be a member of that collective. Identity is not the same thing as the fact of membership in a collective; it is, rather, a form of self-definition, facilitated by images of what we wish our membership in the collective to mean. In this sense, the images we identify with may reflect the aspirations of the collective more than they reflect reality, and their content can vary with shifts in those aspirations.

But the process of identification is usually dialectical. It is just as necessary to say what we are *not* as it is to say what we are—so that, finally, identification comes about by embracing a polarity of positive and negative images. To identify as middle-class, for example, I must have both positive and negative images of what being middle-class entails; then I will know what I should and should not be doing in order to be middle-class. The same goes for racial identity. In the racially turbulent sixties the polarity of images that came to define racial identification was very antagonistic to the polarity that defined middle-class identification. One might say that the positive images of one lined up with the negative images of the other, so that to identify with both required either a contortionist's flexibility or a dangerous splitting of the self. The double bind of the black middle class was in place.

The black middle class has always defined its class identity by means of positive images gleaned from middle- and upper-class white society and by means of negative images of lower-class blacks. This habit goes back to the institution of slavery itself, when "house" slaves both mimicked the whites they served and held themselves above the "field" slaves. But, in the sixties, the old bourgeois impulse to dissociate from the lower classes (the we/they distinction) backfired when racial identity suddenly called for the celebration of this same black lower class. One of the qualities of a double bind is that one feels it more than sees it, and I distinctly remember the tension and strange sense of dishonesty I felt in those days as I moved back and forth like a bigamist between the demands of class and race.

Though my father was born poor, he achieved middle-class standing through much hard work and sacrifice (one of his favorite words) and by identifying fully with solid middle-class values—mainly hard work, family life, property ownership, and education for his children (all four of whom have advanced degrees). In his mind these were not so much values as laws of nature. People who embodied them made up the positive images in his class polarity. The negative images came largely from the blacks he had left behind because they were "going nowhere."

No one in my family remembers how it happened, but as time went on, the negative images congealed into an imaginary character named Sam who, from the extensive service we put him to, quickly grew to mythic proportions. In our family lore he was sometimes a trickster, sometimes a boob, but always possessed of a catalogue of sly faults that gave up graphic images of everything we should not be. On sacrifice: "Sam never thinks about tomorrow. He wants it now or he doesn't care about it." On work: "Sam doesn't favor it too much." On children: "Sam likes to have them but not to raise them." On money: "Sam drinks it up and pisses it out." On fidelity: "Sam has to have two or three women." On clothes: "Sam features loud clothes. He likes to see and be seen." And so on. Sam's persona amounted to a negative instruction manual in class identity.

I don't think that any of us believed Sam's faults were accurate representations of lower-class black life. He was an instrument of self-definition, not of sociological accuracy. It never occurred to us that he looked very much like the white racist stereotype of blacks, or that he might have been a manifestation of our own racial self-hatred. He simply gave us a counterpoint against which to express our aspirations.

If self-hatred was a factor, it was not, for us, a matter of hating lower-class blacks but of hating what we did not want to be.

Still, hate or love aside, it is fundamentally true that my middle-class identity involved a dissociation from images of lower-class black life and a corresponding identification with values and patterns of responsibility that are common to the middle class everywhere. These values sent me a clear message: Be both an individual and a responsible citizen, understand that the quality of your life will approximately reflect the quality of effort you put into it, know that individual responsibility is the basis of freedom, and that the limitations imposed by fate (whether fair or unfair) are no excuse for passivity.

Whether I live up to these values or not, I know that my acceptance of them is the result of lifelong conditioning. I know also that I share this conditioning with middle-class people of all races and that I can no more easily be free of it than I can be free of my race. Whether all this got started because the black middle class modeled itself on the white middle class is no longer relevant. For the middle-class black, conditioned by these values from birth, the sense of meaning they provide is as immutable as the color of his skin.

I started the sixties in high school feeling that my class-conditioning was the surest way to overcome racial barriers. My racial identity was pretty much taken for granted. After all, it was obvious to the world that I was black. Yet I ended the sixties in graduate school a little embarrassed by my class background and with an almost desperate need to be "black." The tables had turned. I knew very clearly (though I struggled to repress it) that my aspirations and my sense of how to operate in the world came from my class background, yet "being black" required certain attitudes and stances that made me feel, secretly, a little duplicitous. The inner compatibility of class and race I had known in 1960 was gone.

For blacks, the decade between 1960 and 1969 saw racial identification undergo the same sort of transformation that national identity undergoes in times of war. It became more self-conscious, more narrowly focused, more prescribed, less tolerant of opposition. It spawned an implicit party line that tended to disallow competing forms of identity. Race-as-identity was lifted from the relative slumber it knew in the fifties and pressed into service in a social and political war against oppression. It was redefined along sharp adversarial lines and directed toward the goal of mobilizing the great mass of black Americans in this warlike effort. It was imbued with strong moral authority, useful for denouncing those who opposed it and for celebrating those who honored it as a positive achievement rather than a mere birthright.

The form of racial identification that quickly evolved to meet this challenge presented blacks as a racial monolith, a singular people with a common experience of oppression. Differences within the race, no matter how ineradicable, had to be minimized. Class distinctions were one of the first such differences to be sacrificed, since they not only threatened racial unity but also seemed to stand in contradiction to the principle of equality, which was the announced goal of the movement for racial progress. The discomfort I felt in 1969, the vague but relentless sense of duplicity, was the result of a historical necessity that put my class and race at odds, that was asking me to cast aside the distinction of my class and identify with a monolithic view of my race.

If the form of this racial identity was the monolith, its

substance was victimization. The civil rights movement and the more radical splinter groups of the late sixties were all dedicated to ending racial victimization, and the form of black identity that emerged to facilitate this goal made blackness and victimization virtually synonymous. Since it was our victimization more than any other variable that identified and unified us, it followed logically that the purest black was the poor black. It was images of him that clustered around the positive pole of the race polarity; all other blacks were, in effect, required to identify with him in order to confirm their own blackness.

Certainly, there were more dimensions to the black experience than victimization, but no other had the same capacity to fire the indignation needed for war. So, again out of historical necessity, victimization became the overriding focus of racial identity. But this only deepened the double bind for middle-class blacks like me. When it came to class we were accustomed to defining ourselves against lower-class blacks and identifying with at least the values of middle-class whites; when it came to race we were now being asked to identify with images of lower-class blacks and to see whites, middle-class or otherwise, as victimizers. Negative lining up with positive, we were called upon to reject what we had previously embraced and to embrace what we had previously rejected. To put it still more personally, the Sam figure I had been raised to define myself against had now become the "real" black I was expected to identify with.

The fact that the poor black's new status was only passively earned by the condition of his victimization, not by assertive, positive action, made little difference. Status was status apart from the means by which it was achieved, and along with it came a certain power—the power to define the terms of access to that status, to say who was black and who was not. If a lower-class black said you were not really "black"—a sellout, an Uncle Tom—the judgment was all the more devastating because it carried the authority of his status. And this judgment soon enough came to be accepted by many whites as well.

In graduate school I was once told by a white professor, "Well, but . . . you're not really black. I mean, you're not disadvantaged." In his mind my lack of victim status disqualified me from the race itself.

To overcome marginal status, the middle-class black had to identify with a degree of victimization that was beyond his actual experience. In college (and well beyond) we used to play a game called "nap matching." It was a game of one-upmanship, in which we sat around outdoing each other with stories of racial victimization, symbolically measured by the naps of our hair. Most of us were middle-class, and so had few personal stories to relate, but if we could not match naps with our own biographies, we would move on to those legendary tales of victimization that came to us from the public domain.

The single story that sat atop the pinnacle of racial victimization for us was that of Emmett Till, the Northern black teenager who, on a visit to the South in 1955, was killed and grotesquely mutilated for supposedly looking at or whistling at (we were never sure which, though we argued the point endlessly) a white woman. Oh, how we probed his story, finding in his youth and Northern upbringing the quintessential embodiment of black innocence brought down by a white evil so portentous and apocalyptic, so gnarled and hideous, that it left us with a feeling not far from awe. By telling his story and others like it, we came to *feel* the immutability of our victimization, its utter indigenousness, as a thing on this earth like dirt or sand or water.

Of course, these sessions were a ritual of group identification, a means by which we, as middle-class blacks, could be at one with our race. But why were we, who had only a moderate experience of victimization (and that offset by opportunities our parents never had), so intent on assimilating or appropriating an identity that in so many ways contradicted our own? Because, I think, the sense of innocence that is always entailed in feeling victimized filled us with a corresponding feeling of entitlement, or even license, that helped us endure our vulnerability on a largely white college campus.

In my junior year in college I rode to a debate tournament with three white students and our faculty coach, an elderly English professor. The experience of being the lone black in a group of whites was so familiar to me that I thought nothing of it as our trip began. But then, halfway through the trip, the professor casually turned to me and, in an isn't-the-world-funny sort of tone, said that he had just refused to rent an apartment in a house he owned to a "very nice" black couple because their color would "offend" the white couple who lived downstairs. His eyebrows lifted helplessly over his hawkish nose, suggesting that he too, like me, was a victim of America's racial farce. His look assumed a kind of comradeship: he and I were above this grimy business of race, though for expediency we had occasionally to concede the world its madness.

My vulnerability in this situation came not so much from the professor's blindness to his own racism as from his assumption that I would participate in it, that I would conspire with him against my own race so that he might remain comfortably blind. Why did he think I would be amenable to this? I can only guess that he assumed my middle-class identity was so complete and all-encompassing that I would see his action as nothing more than a trifling concession to the folkways of our land; that I would in fact applaud his decision not to disturb propriety. Blind to both his own racism and to me—one blindness serving the other—he could not recognize that he was asking me to betray my race in the name of my class.

His blindness made me feel vulnerable because it threatened to expose my own repressed ambivalence. His comment pressured me to choose between my class identification, which had contributed to my being a college student and a member of the debating team, and my desperate desire to be "black." I could have one but not both; I was double-bound.

Because double binds are repressed, there is always an element of terror in them: the terror of bringing to the conscious mind the buried duplicity, self-deception, and pretense involved in serving two masters. This terror is the stuff of vulnerability, and since vulnerability is one of the least tolerable of all human feelings, we usually transform it into an emotion that seems to restore the control of which it has robbed us; most often, that emotion is anger. And so, before the professor had even finished his little story, I had become a furnace of rage. The year was 1967, and I had been primed by endless hours of nap-matching to feel, at least consciously, completely at one with the victim-focused black identity. This identity gave me the license, and the impunity, to unleash upon this professor one of those volcanic eruptions of racial indignation familiar to us from the novels of Richard Wright. Like Cross Damon in *The Outsider*, who kills in perfectly righteous anger, I tried to annihilate the man. I punished him, not according to the measure of his crime, but according to the measure of my vulnerability, a measure set by the cumulative tension of years of repressed terror. Soon, I saw that terror in *his* face as he stared black-eyed at the road ahead. My white friends in the backseat, knowing no conflict between their own class and race, were astonished that someone they had taken to be so much like themselves could harbor a rage that for all the world looked murderous.

Though my rage was triggered by the professor's comment, it was deepened and sustained by a complex of need, conflict, and repression in myself of which I had been wholly unaware. Out of my racial vulnerability I had developed the strong need of an identity with which to defend myself. The only such identity available was that of me as victim, him as victimizer. Once in the grip of this paradigm, I began to do far more damage to myself than he had done.

Seeing myself as a victim meant that I clung all the harder to my racial identity, which, in turn, meant that I suppressed my class identity. This cut me off from all the resources my class values might have offered me. In those values, for instance, I might have found the means to a more dispassionate response, the response less of a victim attacked by a victimizer than of an individual offended by a foolish old man. As an individual, I might have reported this professor to the college dean. Or, I might have calmly tried to reveal his blindness to him, and possibly won a convert. (The flagrancy of his remark suggested a hidden guilt and even a self-recognition on which I might have capitalized. Doesn't confession usually signal a willingness to face oneself?) Or I might have simply chuckled and then let my silence serve as an answer to his provocation. Would not my composure, in any form it might take, deflect into his own heart the arrow he'd shot at me?

Instead, my anger, itself the hair-trigger expression of a long-repressed double bind, not only cut me off from the best of my own resources, it also distorted the nature of my true racial problem. The righteousness of this anger and the easy catharsis it brought buoyed the delusion of my victimization and left me as blind as the professor himself.

As a middle-class black I have often felt myself *contriving* to be "black." And I have noticed this same contrivance in others—a certain stretching away from the natural flow of one's life to align oneself with a victim-focused black identity. Our particular needs are out of sync with the form of identity available to meet those needs. Middle-class blacks need to identify racially; it is better to think of ourselves as black and victimized than not black at all; so we contrive (more unconsciously than consciously) to fit ourselves into an identity that denies our class and fails to address the true source of our vulnerability.

For me, this once meant spending inordinate amounts of time at black faculty meetings, though these meetings had little to do with my real racial anxieties or my professional life. I was new to the university, one of two blacks in an English department of over seventy, and I felt a little isolated and vulnerable, though I did not admit it to myself. But at these meetings we discussed the problems of black faculty and students within a framework of victimization. The real vulnerability we felt was covered over by all the adversarial drama the victim/victimizer polarity inspired, and hence went unseen and unassuaged. And this, I think, explains our rather chronic ineffectiveness as a group. Since victimization was not our primary problem—the university had long ago opened its doors to us—we had to contrive to make it so, and there is not much energy in contrivance. What I got at these meetings was ultimately an object lesson in how fruitless struggle can be when it is not grounded in actual need.

At our black faculty meetings, the old equation of blackness with victimization was ever present—to be black was to be a victim; therefore, not to be a victim was not to be black. As we contrived to meet the terms of this formula, there was an inevitable distortion of both ourselves and the larger university. Through the prism of victimization, the university seemed more impenetrable than it actually was, and we more limited in our powers. We fell prey to the victim's myopia, making the university an institution from which we could seek redress, but which we could never fully join. This mind-set often led us to look more for compensations for our supposed victimization than for opportunities we could pursue as individuals.

The discomfort and vulnerability felt by middle-class blacks in the sixties, it could be argued, was a worthwhile price to pay considering the progress achieved during that time of racial confrontation. But what might have been tolerable then is intolerable now. Though changes in American society have made it an anachronism, the monolithic form of racial identification that came out of the sixties is still very much with us. It may be more loosely held, and its power to punish heretics has probably diminished, but it continues to catch middle-class blacks in a double bind, thus impeding not only their own advancement but even, I would contend, that of blacks as a group.

The victim-focused black identity encourages the individual to feel that his advancement depends almost entirely on that of the group. Thus he loses sight not only of his own possibilities but of the inextricable connection between individual effort and individual advancement. This is a profound encumbrance today, when there is more opportunity for blacks than ever before, for it reimposes limitations that can have the same oppressive effect as those the society has only recently begun to remove.

It was the emphasis on mass action in the sixties that made the victim-focused black identity a necessity. But in the nineties and beyond, when racial advancement will come only through a multitude of individual advancements, this form of identity inadvertently adds itself to the forces that hold us back. Hard work, education, individual initiative, stable family life, property ownership—these have always been the means by which ethnic groups have moved ahead in America. Regardless of past or present victimization, these "laws" of advancement apply absolutely to black Americans also. There is no getting around this. What we need is a form of racial identity that energizes the individual by putting him in touch with both his possibilities and his responsibilities.

It has always annoyed me to hear from the mouths of certain arbiters of blackness that middle-class blacks should "reach back" and pull up those blacks less fortunate than they—as though middle-class status was an unearned and essentially passive condition in which one needed a large measure of noblesse oblige to occupy one's time. My own image is of reaching back from a moving train to lift on board those who have no tickets. A noble enough sentiment—but might it not be wiser to show them the entire structure of principles, effort, and sacrifice that puts one in a position to buy a ticket anytime one likes? This, I think, is something members of the black middle class can realistically offer to other blacks. Their example is not only a testament to possibility but also a lesson in method. But they cannot lead by example until they are released from a black identity that regards that example as suspect, that sees them as "marginally" black; indeed that holds *them* back by catching them in a double bind.

To move beyond the victim-focused black identity, we must learn to make a difficult but crucial distinction: between actual victimization, which we must resist with every resource, and identification with the victim's status. Until we do this, we will continue to wrestle more with ourselves than with the new opportunities that so many paid so dearly to win.

7

Affirmative Action

—■—

T h e   P r i c e   o f   P r e f e r e n c e

In a few short years, when my two children will be applying
to college, the affirmative action policies by which most universities offer black students some form of preferential treatment will present me with a dilemma. I am a middle-class
black, a college professor, far from wealthy, but also well-
removed from the kind of deprivation that would qualify my
children for the label "disadvantaged." Both of them have
endured racial insensitivity from whites. They have been
called names, have suffered slights, and have experienced
firsthand the peculiar malevolence that racism brings out in
people. Yet, they have never experienced racial discrimination, have never been stopped by their race on any path
they have chosen to follow. Still, their society now tells them
that if they will only designate themselves as black on their
college applications, they will likely do better in the college
lottery than if they conceal this fact. I think there is something
of a Faustian bargain in this.

Of course, many blacks and a considerable number of whites would say that I was sanctimoniously making affirmative action into a test of character. They would say that this small preference is the meagerest recompense for centuries of unrelieved oppression. And to these arguments other very obvious facts must be added. In America, many marginally competent or flatly incompetent whites are hired everyday—some because their white skin suits the conscious or unconscious racial preference of their employer. The white children of alumni are often grandfathered into elite universities in what can only be seen as a residual benefit of historic white privilege. Worse, white incompetence is always an individual matter, while for blacks it is often confirmation of ugly stereotypes. The Peter Principle was not conceived with only blacks in mind. Given that unfairness cuts both ways, doesn't it only balance the scales of history that my children now receive a slight preference over whites? Doesn't this repay, in a small way, the systematic denial under which their grandfather lived out his days?

So, in theory, affirmative action certainly has all the moral symmetry that fairness requires—the injustice of historical and even contemporary white advantage is offset with black advantage; preference replaces prejudice, inclusion answers exclusion. It is reformist and corrective, even repentent and redemptive. And I would never sneer at these good intentions. Born in the late forties in Chicago, I started my education (a charitable term in this case) in a segregated school and suffered all the indignities that come to blacks in a segregated society. My father, born in the South, only made it to the third grade before the white man's fields took permanent priority over his formal education. And though he educated himself into an advanced reader with an almost professorial authority, he could only drive a truck for a living and never earned more than ninety dollars a week in his entire life. So yes, it is crucial to my sense of citizenship, to my ability to identify with the spirit and the interests of America, to know that this country, however imperfectly, recognizes its past sins and wishes to correct them.

Yet good intentions, because of the opportunity for innocence they offer us, are very seductive and can blind us to the effects they generate when implemented. In our society, affirmative action is, among other things, a testament to white goodwill and to black power, and in the midst of these heavy investments, its effects can be hard to see. But after twenty years of implementation, I think affirmative action has shown itself to be more bad than good and that blacks—whom I will focus on in this essay—now stand to lose more from it than they gain.

In talking with affirmative action administrators and with blacks and whites in general, it is clear that supporters of affirmative action focus on its good intentions while detractors emphasize its negative effects. Proponents talk about "diversity" and "pluralism"; opponents speak of "reverse discrimination," the unfairness of quotas and set-asides. It was virtually impossible to find people outside either camp. The closest I came was a white male manager at a large computer company who said, "I think it amounts to reverse discrimination, but I'll put up with a little of that for a little more diversity." I'll live with a little of the effect to gain a little of the intention, he seemed to be saying. But this only makes him a halfhearted supporter of affirmative action. I think many people who don't really like affirmative action support it to one degree or another anyway.

I believe they do this because of what happened to white

and black Americans in the crucible of the sixties when whites were confronted with their racial guilt and blacks tasted their first real power. In this stormy time white absolution and black power coalesced into virtual mandates for society. Affirmative action became a meeting ground for these mandates in the law, and in the late sixties and early seventies it underwent a remarkable escalation of its mission from simple anti-discrimination enforcement to social engineering by means of quotas, goals, timetables, set-asides and other forms of preferential treatment.

Legally, this was achieved through a series of executive orders and EEOC guidelines that allowed racial imbalances in the workplace to stand as proof of racial discrimination. Once it could be assumed that discrimination explained racial imbalances, it became easy to justify group remedies to presumed discrimination, rather than the normal case-by-case redress for proven discrimination. Preferential treatment through quotas, goals, and so on is designed to correct imbalances based on the assumption that they always indicate discrimination. This expansion of what constitutes discrimination allowed affirmative action to escalate into the business of social engineering in the name of anti-discrimination, to push society toward statistically proportionate racial representation, without any obligation of proving actual discrimination.

What accounted for this shift, I believe, was the white mandate to achieve a new racial innocence and the black mandate to gain power. Even though blacks had made great advances during the sixties without quotas, these mandates, which came to a head in the very late sixties, could no longer be satisfied by anything less than racial preferences. I don't think these mandates in themselves were wrong, since whites clearly needed to do better by blacks and blacks needed more real power in society. But, as they came together in affirmative action, their effect was to distort our understanding of racial discrimination in a way that allowed us to offer the remediation of preference on the basis of mere color rather than actual injury. By making black the color of preference, these mandates have reburdened society with the very marriage of color and preference (in reverse) that we set out to eradicate. The old sin is reaffirmed in a new guise.

But the essential problem with this form of affirmative action is the way it leaps over the hard business of developing a formerly oppressed people to the point where they can achieve proportionate representation on their own (given equal opportunity) and goes straight for the proportionate representation. This may satisfy some whites of their innocence and some blacks of their power, but it does very little to truly uplift blacks.

A white female affirmative action officer at an Ivy League university told me what many supporters of affirmative action now say: "We're after diversity. We ideally want a student body where racial and ethnic groups are represented according to their proportion in society." When affirmative action escalated into social engineering, diversity became a golden word. It grants whites an egalitarian fairness (innocence) and blacks an entitlement to proportionate representation (power). *Diversity* is a term that applies democratic principles to races and cultures rather than to citizens, despite the fact that there is nothing to indicate that real diversity is the same thing as proportionate representation. Too often the result of this on campuses (for example) has been a democracy of colors rather than of people, an artificial diversity that gives the appearance of an educational parity between black and white students that has not yet been achieved in reality. Here again, racial preferences allow society to leapfrog over the difficult problem of developing blacks to parity with whites and into a cosmetic diversity that covers the blemish of disparity—a full six years after admission, only about 26 percent of black students graduate from college.

Racial representation is not the same thing as racial development, yet affirmative action fosters a confusion of these very different needs. Representation can be manufactured; development is always hard-earned. However, it is the music of innocence and power that we hear in affirmative action that causes us to cling to it and to its distracting emphasis on representation. The fact is that after twenty years of racial preferences, the gap between white and black median income is greater than it was in the seventies. None of this is to say that blacks don't need policies that ensure our right to equal opportunity, but what we need more is the development that will let us take advantage of society's efforts to include us.

I think that one of the most troubling effects of racial preferences for blacks is a kind of demoralization, or put another way, an enlargement of self-doubt. Under affirmative action the quality that earns us preferential treatment is an implied inferiority. However this inferiority is explained—and it is easily enough explained by the myriad deprivations that grew out of our oppression—it is still inferiority. There are explanations, and then there is the fact. And the fact must be borne by the individual as a condition apart from the explanation, apart even from the fact that others like himself also bear this condition. In integrated situations where blacks must compete with whites who may be better prepared, these explanations may quickly wear thin and expose the individual to racial as well as personal self-doubt.

All of this is compounded by the cultural myth of black inferiority that blacks have always lived with. What this means in practical terms is that when blacks deliver themselves into integrated situations, they encounter a nasty little reflex in whites, a mindless, atavistic reflex that responds to the color black with alarm. Attributions may follow this alarm if the white cares to indulge them, and if they do, they will most likely be negative—one such attribution is intellectual ineptness. I think this reflex and the attributions that may follow it embarrass most whites today, therefore, it is usually quickly repressed. Nevertheless, on an equally atavistic level, the black will be aware of the reflex his color triggers and will feel a stab of horror at seeing himself reflected in this way. He, too, will do a quick repression, but a lifetime of such stabbings is what constitutes his inner realm of racial doubt.

The effects of this may be a subject for another essay. The point here is that the implication of inferiority that racial preferences engender in both the white and black mind expands rather than contracts this doubt. Even when the black sees no implication of inferiority in racial preferences, he knows that whites do, so that—consciously or unconsciously—the result is virtually the same. The effect of preferential treatment—the lowering of normal standards to increase black representation—puts blacks at war with an expanded realm of debilitating doubt, so that the doubt itself becomes an unrecognized preoccupation that undermines their ability to perform, especially in integrated situations. On largely white campuses, blacks are five times more likely to drop out than whites. Preferential treatment, no matter how it is justified in the light of day, subjects blacks to a midnight of self-doubt, and so often transforms their advantage into a revolving door.

Another liability of affirmative action comes from the fact that it indirectly encourages blacks to exploit their own past victimization as a source of power and privilege. Victimization, like implied inferiority, is what justifies preference, so that to receive the benefits of preferential treatment one must, to some extent, become invested in the view of one's self as a victim. In this way, affirmative action nurtures a victim-focused identity in blacks. The obvious irony here is that we become inadvertently invested in the very condition we are trying to overcome. Racial preferences send us the message that there is more power in our past suffering than our present achievements—none of which could bring us a *preference* over others.

When power itself grows out of suffering, then blacks are encouraged to expand the boundaries of what qualifies as racial oppression, a situation that can lead us to paint our victimization in vivid colors, even as we receive the benefits of preference. The same corporations and institutions that give us preference are also seen as our oppressors. At Stanford University minority students—some of whom enjoy as much as $15,000 a year in financial aid—recently took over the president's office demanding, among other things, more financial aid. The power to be found in victimization, like any power, is intoxicating and can lend itself to the creation of a new class of super-victims who can feel the pea of victimization under twenty mattresses. Preferential treatment rewards us for being underdogs rather than for moving beyond that status—a misplacement of incentives that, along with its deepening of our doubt, is more a yoke than a spur.

But, I think, one of the worst prices that blacks pay for preference has to do with an illusion. I saw this illusion at work recently in the mother of a middle-class black student who was going off to his first semester of college. "They owe us this, so don't think for a minute that you don't belong there." This is the logic by which many blacks, and some whites, justify affirmative action—it is something "owed," a form of reparation. But this logic overlooks a much harder and less digestible reality, that it is impossible to repay blacks living today for the historic suffering of the race. If all blacks were given a million dollars tomorrow morning it would not amount to a dime on the dollar of three centuries of oppression, nor would it obviate the residues of that oppression that we still carry today. The concept of historic reparation grows out of man's need to impose a degree of justice on the world that simply does not exist. Suffering can be endured and overcome, it cannot be repaid. Blacks cannot be repaid for the injustice done to the race, but we can be corrupted by society's guilty gestures of repayment.

Affirmative action is such a gesture. It tells us that racial preferences can do for us what we cannot do for ourselves. The corruption here is in the hidden incentive *not* to do what we believe preferences will do. This is an incentive to be reliant on others just as we are struggling for self-reliance. And it keeps alive the illusion that we can find some deliverance in repayment. The hardest thing for any sufferer to accept is that his suffering excuses him from very little and never has enough currency to restore him. To think otherwise is to prolong the suffering.

Several blacks I spoke with said they were still in favor of affirmative action because of the "subtle" discrimination blacks were subject to once on the job. One photojournalist said, "They have ways of ignoring you." A black female television producer said, "You can't file a lawsuit when your boss doesn't invite you to the insider meetings without ruining your career. So we still need affirmative action." Others mentioned the infamous "glass ceiling" through which blacks can see the top positions of authority but never reach them. But I don't think racial preferences are a protection against this subtle discrimination; I think they contribute to it.

In any workplace, racial preferences will always create two-tiered populations composed of preferreds and unpreferreds. This division makes automatic a perception of enhanced competence for the unpreferreds and of questionable competence for the preferreds—the former earned his way, even though others were given preference, while the latter made it by color as much as by competence. Racial preferences implicitly mark whites with an exaggerated superiority just as they mark blacks with an exaggerated inferiority. They not only reinforce America's oldest racial myth but, for blacks, they have the effect of stigmatizing the already stigmatized.

I think that much of the "subtle" discrimination that blacks talk about is often (not always) discrimination against the stigma of questionable competence that affirmative action delivers to blacks. In this sense, preferences scapegoat the very people they seek to help. And it may be that at a certain level employers impose a glass ceiling, but this may not be against the race so much as against the race's reputation for having advanced by color as much as by competence. Affirmative action makes a glass ceiling virtually necessary as a protection against the corruptions of preferential treatment. This ceiling is the point at which corporations shift the emphasis from color to competency and stop playing the affirmative action game. Here preference backfires for blacks and becomes a taint that holds them back. Of course, one could argue that this taint, which is, after all, in the minds of whites, becomes nothing more than an excuse to discriminate against blacks. And certainly the result is the same in either case —blacks don't get past the glass ceiling. But this argument does not get around the fact that racial preferences now taint this color with a new theme of suspicion that makes it even more vulnerable to the impulse in others to discriminate. In this crucial yet gray area of perceived competence, preferences make whites look better than they are and blacks worse, while doing nothing whatever to stop the very real discrimination that blacks may encounter. I don't wish to justify the glass ceiling here, but only to suggest the very subtle ways that affirmative action revives rather than extinguishes the old rationalizations for racial discrimination.

In education, a revolving door; in employment, a glass ceiling.

I believe affirmative action is problematic in our society because it tries to function like a social program. Rather than ask it to ensure equal opportunity we have demanded that it create parity between the races. But preferential treatment does not teach skills, or educate, or instill motivation. It only passes out entitlement by color, a situation that in my profession has created an unrealistically high demand for black professors. The social engineer's assumption is that this high demand will inspire more blacks to earn Ph.D.'s and join the profession. In fact, the number of blacks earning Ph.D.'s has declined in recent years. A Ph.D. must be developed from preschool on. He requires family and community support. He must acquire an entire system of values that enables him to work hard while delaying gratification. There are social programs, I believe, that can (and should) help blacks *develop* in all these areas, but entitlement by color is not a social program; it is a dubious reward for being black.

It now seems clear that the Supreme Court, in a series of recent decisions, is moving away from racial preferences. It has disallowed preferences except in instances of "identified discrimination," eroded the precedent that statistical racial imbalances are *prima facie* evidence of discrimination, and in effect granted white males the right to challenge consent degrees that use preference to achieve racial balances in the workplace. One civil rights leader said, "Night has fallen on civil rights." But I am not so sure. The effect of these decisions is to protect the constitutional rights of everyone rather than take rights away from blacks. What they do take away from blacks is the special entitlement to more rights than others that preferences always grant. Night has fallen on racial preferences, not on the fundamental rights of black Americans. The reason for this shift, I believe, is that the white mandate for absolution from past racial sins has weakened considerably during the eighties. Whites are now less willing to endure unfairness to themselves in order to grant special entitlements to blacks, even when these entitlements are justified in the name of past suffering. Yet the black mandate for more power in society has remained unchanged. And I think part of the anxiety that many blacks feel over these decisions has to do with the loss of black power they may signal. We had won a certain specialness and now we are losing it.

But the power we've lost by these decisions is really only the power that grows out of our victimization—the power to claim special entitlements under the law because of past oppression. This is not a very substantial or reliable power, and it is important that we know this so we can focus more exclusively on the kind of development that will bring enduring power. There is talk now that Congress will pass new legislation to compensate for these new limits on affirmative action. If this happens, I hope that their focus will be on development and anti-discrimination rather than entitlement, on achieving racial parity rather than jerry-building racial diversity.

I would also like to see affirmative action go back to its original purpose of enforcing equal opportunity—a purpose that in itself disallows racial preferences. We cannot be sure that the discriminatory impulse in America has yet been shamed into extinction, and I believe affirmative action can make its greatest contribution by providing a rigorous vigilance in this area. It can guard constitutional rather than racial rights, and help institutions evolve standards of merit and selection that are appropriate to the institution's needs yet as free of racial bias as possible (again, with the understanding that racial imbalances are not always an indication of racial bias). One of the most important things affirmative action can do is to define exactly what racial discrimination is and how it might manifest itself within a specific institution. The impulse to discriminate *is* subtle and cannot be ferreted out unless its many guises are made clear to people. Along with this there should be monitoring of institutions and heavy sanctions brought to bear when actual discrimination is found. This is the sort of affirmative action that America owes to blacks and to itself. It goes after the evil of discrimination itself, while preferences only sidestep the evil and grant entitlement to its *presumed* victims.

But if not preferences, then what? I think we need social policies that are committed to two goals: the educational and economic development of disadvantaged people, regardless of race, and the eradication from our society—through close monitoring and severe sanctions—of racial, ethnic, or gender discrimination. Preferences will not deliver us to either of these goals, since they tend to benefit those who are not disadvantaged—middle-class white women and middle-class blacks—and attack one form of discrimination with another. Preferences are inexpensive and carry the glamour of good intentions—change the numbers and the good deed is done. To be against them is to be unkind. But I think the unkindest cut is to bestow on children like my own an undeserved advantage while neglecting the development of those disadvantaged children on the East Side of my city who will likely never be in a position to benefit from a preference. Give my children fairness; give disadvantaged children a better shot at development—better elementary and secondary schools, job training, safer neighborhoods, better financial assistance for college, and so on. Fewer blacks go to college today than ten years ago; more black males of college age are in prison or under the control of the criminal justice system than in college. This despite racial preferences.

The mandates of black power and white absolution out of which preferences emerged were not wrong in themselves. What was wrong was that both races focused more on the goals of these mandates than on the means to the goals. Blacks can have no real power without taking responsibility for their own educational and economic development. Whites can have no racial innocence without earning it by eradicating discrimination and helping the disadvantaged to develop. Because we ignored the means, the goals have not been reached, and the real work remains to be done.

8

The Recoloring
of Campus Life

■

Student Racism,
Academic Pluralism, and
the End of a Dream

In the past few years, we have witnessed what the National Institute Against Prejudice and Violence calls a "proliferation" of racial incidents on college campuses around the country. Incidents of on-campus "intergroup conflict" have occurred at more than 160 colleges in the last two years, according to the institute. The nature of these incidents has ranged from open racial violence—most notoriously, the October 1986 beating of a black student at the University of Massachusetts at Amherst after an argument about the World Series turned into a racial bashing, with a crowd of up to three thousand whites chasing twenty blacks—to the harassment of minority students and acts of racial or ethnic insensitivity, with by far the greatest number of episodes falling in the last two categories. At Yale last year, a swastika and the words "white power" were painted on the university's Afro-American cultural center. Racist jokes were aired not long ago on a campus radio station at the University of Michigan. And at the University of Wisconsin at Madison, members of the Zeta Beta Tau fraternity held a mock slave auction in which pledges painted their faces black and wore Afro wigs. Two weeks after the president of Stanford University informed the incoming freshmen class last fall that "bigotry is out, and I mean it," two freshmen defaced a poster of Beethoven—gave the image thick lips—and hung it on a black student's door.

In response, black students around the country have rediscovered the militant protest strategies of the sixties. At the University of Massachusetts at Amherst, Williams College, Penn State University, University of California–Berkeley, UCLA, Stanford University, and countless other campuses, black students have sat in, marched, and rallied. But much of what they were marching and rallying about seemed less a response to specific racial incidents than a call for broader action on the part of the colleges and universities they were attending. Black students have demanded everything from more black faculty members and new courses on racism to the addition of "ethnic" foods in the cafeteria. There is the sense in these demands that racism runs deep. Is the campus becoming the battleground for a renewed war between the races? I don't think so, not really. But if it is not a war, the problem of campus racism does represent a new and surprising hardening of racial lines within the most traditionally liberal and tolerant of America's institutions—its universities.

As a black who has spent his entire adult life on predominantly white campuses, I found it hard to believe that the problem of campus racism was as dramatic as some of the incidents seemed to make it. The incidents I read or heard about often seemed prankish and adolescent, though not necessarily harmless. There is a meanness in them but not much menace; no one is proposing to reinstitute Jim Crow on campus. On the California campus where I now teach, there have been few signs of racial tension.

And, of course, universities are not where racial problems tend to arise. When I went to college in the mid-sixties, colleges were oases of calm and understanding in a racially tense society; campus life—with its traditions of tolerance and fairness, its very distance from the "real" world—imposed a degree of broad-mindedness on even the most provincial students. If I met whites who were not anxious to be friends with blacks, most were at least vaguely friendly to the cause of our freedom. In any case, there was no guerrilla activity against our presence, no "mine field of racism" (as one black student at Berkeley recently put it to me) to negotiate. I wouldn't say that the phrase "campus racism" is a contradiction in terms, but until recently it certainly seemed an incongruence.

But a greater incongruence is the generational timing of this new problem on the campuses. Today's undergraduates were born after the passage of the 1964 Civil Rights Act. They grew up in an age when racial equality was for the first time enforceable by law. This too was a time when blacks suddenly appeared on television, as mayors of big cities, as icons of popular culture, as teachers, and in some cases even as neighbors. Today's black and white college students, veterans of "Sesame Street" and often of integrated grammar and high schools, have had more opportunities to know each other than any previous generation in American history. Not enough opportunities, perhaps, but enough to make the notion of racial tension on campus something of a mystery, at least to me.

To look at this mystery, I left my own campus with its burden of familiarity and talked with black and white students at California schools where racial incidents had occurred: Stanford, UCLA, and Berkeley. I spoke with black and white students—not with Asians and Hispanics—because, as always, blacks and whites represent the deepest lines of division, and because I hesitate to wander onto the complex territory of other minority groups. A phrase by William H. Gass—"the hidden internality of things"—describes, with maybe a little too much grandeur, what I hoped to find. But it is what I wanted to find, for this is the kind of problem that makes a black person nervous, which is not to say that it doesn't unnerve whites as well. Once every six months or so someone yells "nigger" at me from a passing car. I don't like to think that these solo artists might soon make up a chorus, or worse, that this chorus might one day soon sing to me from the paths of my own campus.

I have long believed that the trouble between the races is seldom what it appears to be. It was not hard to see after my first talks with students that racial tension on campus is a problem that misrepresents itself. It has the same look, the archetypal pattern, of America's timeless racial conflict— white racism and black protest. And I think part of our concern over it comes from the fact that it has the feel of a relapse, illness gone and come again. But if we are seeing the same symptoms, I don't believe we are dealing with the same illness. For one thing, I think racial tension on campus is more the result of racial equality than inequality.

How to live with racial difference has been America's profound social problem. For the first hundred years or so following emancipation it was controlled by a legally sanctioned inequality that kept the races from each other. No longer is this the case. On campuses today, as throughout society, blacks enjoy equality under the law—a profound social advancement. No student may be kept out of a class or a dormitory or an extracurricular activity because of his or her race. But there is a paradox here: on a campus where members of all races are gathered, mixed together in the classroom as well as socially, differences are more exposed than ever. And this is where the trouble starts. For members of each race—young adults coming into their own, often away from home for the first time—bring to this site of freedom, exploration, and (now, today) equality, very deep fears, anxieties, inchoate feelings of racial shame, anger, and guilt. These feelings could lie dormant in the home, in familiar neighborhoods, in simpler days of childhood. But the college campus, with its structures of interaction and adult-level competition—the big exam, the dorm, the mixer—is another matter. I think campus racism is born of the rub between racial difference and a setting, the campus itself, devoted to interaction and equality. On our campuses, such concentrated micro-societies, all that remains unresolved between blacks and whites, all the old wounds and shames that have never been addressed, present themselves for attention—and present our youth with pressures they cannot always handle.

I have mentioned one paradox: racial fears and anxieties among blacks and whites, bubbling up in an era of racial equality under the law, in settings that are among the freest and fairest in society. But there is another, related paradox, stemming from the notion of—and practice of—affirmative action. Under the provisions of the Equal Employment Opportunity Act of 1972, all state governments and institutions (including universities) were forced to initiate plans to increase the proportion of minority and women employees and, in the case of universities, of students too. Affirmative action plans that establish racial quotas were ruled unconstitutional more than ten years ago in *University of California* v. *Bakke*, but such plans are still thought by some to secretly exist, and lawsuits having to do with alleged quotas are still very much with us. But quotas are only the most controversial aspect of affirmative action; the principal of affirmative action is reflected in various university programs aimed at redressing and overcoming past patterns of discrimination. Of course, to be conscious of past patterns of discriminations—the fact, say, that public schools in the black inner cities are more crowded and employ fewer top-notch teachers than a white suburban public school, and that this is a factor in student performance—is only reasonable. But in doing this we also call attention quite obviously to difference: in the case of blacks and whites, racial difference. What has emerged on campus in recent years—as a result of the new equality and of affirmative action and, in a sense, as a result of progress —is a *politics of difference*, a troubling, volatile politics in which each group justifies itself, its sense of worth and its pursuit of power, through difference alone.

In this context, racial, ethnic, and gender differences become forms of sovereignty, campuses become balkanized, and each group fights with whatever means are available. No doubt there are many factors that have contributed to the rise of

racial tension on campus: What has been the role of frater-
nities, which have returned to campus with their inclusions
and exclusions? What role has the heightened notion of college as some first step to personal, financial success played
in increasing competition, and thus tension? But mostly, what
I sense is that in interactive settings, fighting the fights of
"difference," old ghosts are stirred and haunt again. Black
and white Americans simply have the power to make each
other feel shame and guilt. In most situations, we may be
able to deny these feelings, keep them at bay. But these
feelings are likely to surface on college campuses, where
young people are groping for identity and power, and where
difference is made to matter so greatly. In a way, racial tension
on campus in the eighties might have been inevitable.

I would like, first, to discuss black students, their anxieties
and vulnerabilities. The accusation black Americans have
always lived with is that they are inferior—inferior simply
because they are black. And this accusation has been too
uniform, too ingrained in cultural imagery, too enforced by
law, custom, and every form of power not to have left a mark.
Black inferiority was a precept accepted by the founders of
this nation; it was a principle of social organization that relegated blacks to the sidelines of American life. So when young
black students find themselves on white campuses surrounded
by those who have historically claimed superiority, they are
also surrounded by the myth of their inferiority.

Of course, it is true that many young people come to college
with some anxiety about not being good enough. But only
blacks come wearing a color that is still, in the minds of
some, a sign of inferiority. Poles, Jews, Hispanics, and other
groups also endure degrading stereotypes. But two things
make the myth of black inferiority a far heavier burden—the

broadness of its scope and its incarnation in color. There are
not only more stereotypes of blacks than of other groups, but
these stereotypes are also more dehumanizing, more focused
on the most despised human traits: stupidity, laziness, sexual
immorality, dirtiness, and so on. In America's racial and
ethnic hierarchy, blacks have clearly been relegated to the
lowest level—have been burdened with an ambiguous, ani-
malistic humanity. Moreover, this is made unavoidable for
blacks by sheer visibility of black skin, a skin that evokes
the myth of inferiority on sight. Today this myth is sadly
reinforced for many black students by affirmative action programs, under which blacks may often enter college with lower
test scores and high school grade point averages than whites.
"They see me as an affirmative action case," one black student
told me at UCLA. This reinforces the myth of inferiority by
implying that blacks are not good enough to make it into
college on their own.

So when a black student enters college, the myth of inferiority compounds the normal anxiousness over whether he
or she will be good enough. This anxiety is not only personal
but also racial. The families of these students will have
pounded into them the fact that blacks are not inferior. And
probably more than anything it is this pounding that finally
leaves the mark. If I am not inferior, why the need to say
so?

This myth of inferiority constitutes a very sharp and ongoing
anxiety for young blacks, the nature of which is very precise:
it is the terror that somehow, through one's actions or by
virtue of some "proof" (a poor grade, a flubbed response in
class), one's fear of inferiority—inculcated in ways large and
small by society—will be confirmed as real. On a university

campus where intelligence itself is the ultimate measure, this anxiety is bound to be triggered.

A black student I met at UCLA was disturbed a little when I asked him if he ever felt vulnerable—anxious about "black inferiority"—as a black student. But after a long pause, he finally said, "I think I do." The example he gave was of a large lecture class he'd taken with over three hundred students. Fifty or so black students sat in the back of the lecture hall and "acted out every stereotype in the book." They were loud, ate food, came in late—and generally got lower grades than whites in the class. "I knew I would be seen like them, and I didn't like it. I never sat by them." Seen like what, I asked, though we both knew the answer. "As lazy, ignorant, and stupid," he said sadly.

Had the group at the back been white fraternity brothers, they would not have been seen as dumb whites, of course. And a frat brother who worried about his grades would not worry that he been seen "like them." The terror in this situation for the black student I spoke with was that his own deeply buried anxiety would be given credence, that the myth would be verified, and that he would feel shame and humiliation not because of who he was but simply because he was black. In this lecture hall his race, quite apart from his performance, might subject him to four unendurable feelings—diminishment, accountability to the preconceptions of whites, a powerlessness to change those preconceptions, and finally, shame. These are the feelings that make up his racial anxiety, and that of all blacks on any campus. On a white campus a black is never far from these feelings, and even his unconscious knowledge that he is subject to them can undermine his self-esteem. There are blacks on any campus who are not up to doing good college-level work. Certain black students may not be happy or motivated or in the appropriate field of study—*just like whites*. (Let us not forget that many white students get poor grades, fail, drop out.) Moreover, many more blacks than whites are not quite prepared for college, may have to catch up, owing to factors beyond their control: poor previous schooling, for example. But the white who has to catch up will not be anxious that his being behind is a matter of his whiteness, of his being racially inferior. The black student may well have such a fear.

This, I believe, is one reason why black colleges in America turn out 37 percent of all black college graduates though they enroll only 16 percent of black college students. Without whites around on campus, the myth of inferiority is in abeyance and, along with it, a great reservoir of culturally imposed self-doubt. On black campuses, feelings of inferiority are personal; on campuses with a white majority, a black's problems have a way of becoming a "black" problem.

But this feeling of vulnerability a black may feel, in itself, is not as serious a problem as what he or she does with it. To admit that one is made anxious in integrated situations about the myth of racial inferiority is difficult for young blacks. It seems like admitting that one is racially inferior. And so, most often, the student will deny harboring the feelings. This is where some of the pangs of racial tension begin, because denial always involves distortion.

In order to deny a problem we must tell ourselves that the problem is something different from what it really is. A black student at Berkeley told me that he felt defensive every time he walked into a classroom of white faces. When I asked why, he said, "Because I know they're all racists. They think blacks are stupid." Of course it may be true that some whites feel this way, but the singular focus on white racism allows this student to obscure his own underlying racial anxiety. He can now say that his problem—facing a classroom of white faces, *fearing* that they think he is dumb—is entirely the result of certifiable white racism and has nothing to do with his own anxieties, or even that this particular academic subject may not be his best. Now all the terror of his anxiety, its powerful energy, is devoted to simply *seeing* racism. Whatever evidence of racism he finds—and looking this hard, he will no doubt find some—can be brought in to buttress his distorted view of the problem while his actual deep-seated anxiety goes unseen.

Denial, and the distortion that results, places the problem *outside* the self and in the world. It is not that I have any inferiority anxiety because of my race; it is that I am going to school with people who don't like blacks. This is the shift in thinking that allows black students to reenact the protest pattern of the sixties. *Denied racial anxiety–distortion–reenactment* is the process by which feelings of inferiority are transformed into an exaggerated white menace—which is then protested against with the techniques of the past. Under the sway of this process, black students believe that history is repeating itself, that it's just like the sixties, or fifties. In fact, it is not-yet-healed wounds from the past, rather than the inequality that created the wounds, that is the real problem.

This process generates an unconscious need to exaggerate the level of racism on campus—to make it a matter of the system, not just a handful of students. Racism is the avenue away from the true inner anxiety. How many students demonstrating for black theme dorms—demonstrating in the style

of the sixties, when the battle was to win for blacks a place
on campus—might be better off spending their time reading
and studying? Black students have the highest dropout rate
and the lowest grade point average of any group in American
universities. This need not be so. And it is not the result of
not having black theme dorms.

It was my very good fortune to go to college in 1964, when
the question of black "inferiority" was openly talked about
among blacks. The summer before I left for college, I heard
Martin Luther King speak in Chicago, and he laid it on the
line for black students everywhere: "When you are behind
in a footrace, the only way to get ahead is to run faster than
the man in front of you. So when your white roommate says
he's tired and goes to sleep, you stay up and burn the midnight
oil." His statement that we were "behind in a footrace" acknowledged that, because of history, of few opportunities, of
racism, we were, in a sense, "inferior." But this had to do
with what had been done to our parents and their parents,
not with inherent inferiority. And because it was acknowledged, it was presented to us as a challenge rather than a
mark of shame.

Of the eighteen black students (in a student body of one
thousand) who were on campus in my freshman year, all
graduated, though a number of us were not from the middle
class. At the university where I currently teach, the dropout
rate for black students is 72 percent, despite the presence
of several academic support programs, a counseling center
with black counselors, an Afro-American studies department,
black faculty, administrators, and staff, a general education
curriculum that emphasizes "cultural pluralism," an Educational Opportunities Program, a mentor program, a black

faculty and staff association, and an administration and faculty that often announce the need to do more for black students.

It may be unfair to compare my generation with the current one. Parents do this compulsively and to little end but self-congratulation. But I don't congratulate my generation. I think we were advantaged. We came along at a time when racial integration was held in high esteem. And integration was a very challenging social concept for both blacks and whites. We were remaking ourselves—that's what one did at college—and making history. We had something to prove. This was a profound advantage; it gave us clarity and a challenge. Achievement in the American mainstream was the goal of integration, and the best thing about this challenge was its secondary message—that we *could* achieve.

There is much irony in the fact that black power would come along in the late sixties and change all this. Black power was a movement of uplift and pride, and yet it also delivered the weight of pride—a weight that would burden black students from then on. Black power "nationalized" the black identity, made blackness itself an object of celebration, an allegiance. But if it transformed a mark of shame into a mark of pride, it also, in the name of pride, required the denial of racial anxiety. Without a frank account of one's anxieties, there is no clear direction, no concrete challenge. Black students today do not get as clear a message from their racial identity as my generation got. They are not filled with the same urgency to prove themselves because black pride has said, *You're already proven, already equal, as good as anybody.*

The "black identity" shaped by black power most forcefully contributes to racial tensions on campuses by basing entitlement more on race than on constitutional rights and standards of merit. With integration, black entitlement derived from constitutional principles of fairness. Black power changed this by skewing the formula from rights to color—if you were black, you were entitled. Thus the United Coalition Against Racism (UCAR) at the University of Michigan could "demand" two years ago that all black professors be given immediate tenure, that there is a special pay incentive for black professors, and that money be provided for an all-black student union. In this formula, black becomes the very color of entitlement, an extra right in itself, and a very dangerous grandiosity is promoted in which blackness amounts to specialness.

Race is, by any standard, an unprincipled source of power. And on campuses the use of racial power by one group makes racial, ethnic, or gender difference a currency of power for all groups. When I make my *difference* into power, other groups must seize upon their difference to contain my power and maintain their position relative to me. Very quickly a kind of politics of difference emerges in which racial, ethnic, and gender groups are forced to assert their entitlement and vie for power based on the single quality that makes them different from one another.

On many campuses today academic departments and programs are established on the basis of difference—black studies, women's studies, Asian studies, and so on—despite the fact that there is nothing in these "difference" departments that cannot be studied within traditional academic disciplines. If their rationale is truly past exclusion from the mainstream curriculum, shouldn't the goal now be complete inclusion rather than separateness? I think this logic is overlooked because those groups are too interested in the power their difference can bring, and they insist on separate departments and programs as tribute to that power.

This politics of difference makes everyone on campus a member of a minority group. It also makes racial tension inevitable. To highlight one's difference as a source of advantage is also, indirectly, to inspire the enemies of that difference. When blackness (and femaleness) become power, then white maleness is also sanctioned as power. A white male student I spoke with at Stanford said, "One of my friends said the other day that we should get together and start up a white student union and come up with a list of demands."

It is certainly true that white maleness has long been an unfair source of power. But the sin of white male power is precisely its use of race and gender as a source of entitlement. When minorities and women use their race, ethnicity, and gender in the same way, they not only commit the same sin but also, indirectly, sanction the very form of power that oppressed them in the first place. The politics of difference is based on a tit-for-tat sort of logic in which every victory only calls one's enemies to arms.

This elevation of difference undermines the communal impulse by making each group foreign and inaccessible to others. When difference is celebrated rather than remarked, people must think in terms of difference, they must find meaning in difference, and this meaning comes from an endless process of contrasting one's group with other groups. Blacks use whites to define themselves as different, women use men, Hispanics use whites and blacks, and on it goes. And in the process each group mythologizes and mystifies its difference, puts it beyond the full comprehension of outsiders.

Difference becomes inaccessible preciousness toward which outsiders are expected to be simply and uncomprehendingly reverential. But beware: in this world, even the insulated world of the college campus, preciousness is a balloon asking for a needle. At Smith College graffiti appears: "Niggers, spics, and chinks. Quit complaining or get out."

I think that those who run our colleges and universities are every bit as responsible for the politics of difference as are minority students. To correct the exclusions once caused by race and gender, universities—under the banner of affirmative action—have relied too heavily on race and gender as criteria. So rather than break the link between difference and power, they have reinforced it. On most campuses today, a well-to-do black student with two professional parents is qualified by his race for scholarship monies that are not available to a lower-middle-class white student. A white female with a private school education and every form of cultural advantage comes under the affirmative action umbrella. This kind of inequity is an invitation to backlash.

What universities are quite rightly trying to do is compensate people for past discrimination and the deprivations that followed from it. But race and gender alone offer only the grossest measure of this. And the failure of universities has been their backing away from the challenge of identifying principles of fairness and merit that make finer and more equitable distinctions. The real challenge is not simply to include a certain number of blacks, but to end discrimination against all blacks and to offer special help to those with talent who have also been economically deprived.

With regard to black students, affirmative action has led universities to correlate color with poverty and disadvantage in so absolute a way as to encourage the politics of difference. But why have they gone along with this? My belief is that it is due to the specific form of racial anxiety to which whites are most subject.

Most of the white students I talked with spoke as if from under a faint cloud of accusation. There was always a ring of defensiveness in their complaints about blacks. A white student I spoke to at UCLA told me: "Most white students on this campus think the black student leadership here is made up of oversensitive crybabies who spend all their time looking for things to kick up a ruckus about." A white student at Stanford said, "Blacks do nothing but complain and ask for sympathy when everyone really knows that they don't do well because they don't try. If they worked harder, they could do as well as everyone else."

That these students felt accused was most obvious in their compulsion to assure me that they were not racist. Oblique versions of some-of-my-best-friends-are stories came ritualistically before or after critiques of black students. Some said flatly, "I am not a racist, but . . ." Of course, we all deny being racist, but we only do this compulsively, I think, when we are working against an accusation of bias. I think it was the color of my skin itself that accused them.

This was the meta-message that surrounded these conversations like an aura, and it is, I believe, the core of white American racial anxiety. My skin not only accused them; it judged them. And this judgment was a sad gift of history that brought them to account whether they deserved such accountability or not. It said that wherever and whenever blacks were concerned, they had reason to feel guilt. And whether it was earned or unearned, I think it was guilt that set off the compulsion in these students to disclaim. I believe it is true that, in America, black people make white people feel guilty.

Guilt is the essence of white anxiety just as inferiority is the essence of black anxiety. And the terror that it carries for whites is the terror of discovering that one has reason to feel guilt where blacks are concerned—not so much because of what blacks might think but because of what guilt can say about oneself. If the darkest fear of blacks is inferiority, the darkest fear of whites is that their better lot in life is at least partially the result of their capacity for evil—their capacity to dehumanize an entire people for their own benefit and then to be indifferent to the devastation their dehumanization has wrought on successive generations of their victims. This is the terror that whites are vulnerable to regarding blacks. And the mere fact of being white is sufficient to feel it, since even whites with hearts clean of racism benefit from being white —benefit at the expense of blacks. This is a conditional guilt having nothing to do with individual intentions or actions. And it makes for a very powerful anxiety because it threatens whites with a view of themselves as inhuman, just as inferiority threatens blacks with a similar view of themselves. At the dark core of both anxieties is a suspicion of incomplete humanity.

So, the white students I met were not just meeting me; they were also meeting the possibility of their own inhumanity. And this, I think, is what explains how some young white college students in the late eighties could so frankly take part in racially insensitive and outright racist acts. They were expected to be cleaner of racism than any previous generation—they were born into the Great Society. But this expectation overlooks the fact that, for them, color is still an accusation and judgment. In black faces there is a discomforting reflection of white collective shame. Blacks remind them that their racial innocence is questionable, that they are the beneficiaries of past and present racism, and the sins of the father may well have been visited on the children.

And yet young whites tell themselves that they had nothing to do with the oppression of black people. They have a stronger belief in their racial innocence than any previous generation of whites and a natural hostility toward anyone who would challenge that innocence. So (with a great deal of individual variation) they can end up in the paradoxical position of being hostile to blacks as a way of defending their own racial innocence.

I think this is what the young white editors of the *Dartmouth Review* were doing when they harassed black music professor William Cole. Weren't they saying, in effect, I am so free of racial guilt that I can afford to attack blacks ruthlessly and still be racially innocent? The ruthlessness of these attacks was a form of denial, a badge of innocence. The more they were charged with racism, the more ugly and confrontational their harassment became (an escalation unexplained even by the serious charges against Professor Cole). Racism became a means of rejecting racial guilt, a way of showing that they were not, ultimately, racists.

The politics of difference sets up a struggle for innocence among all groups. When difference is the currency of power, each group must fight for the innocence that entitles it to power. To gain this innocence, blacks sting whites with guilt, remind them of their racial past, accuse them of new and more subtle forms of racism. One way whites retrieve their innocence is to discredit blacks and deny their difficulties, for in this denial is the denial of their own guilt. To blacks this denial looks like racism, a racism that feeds black innocence and encourages them to throw more guilt at whites. And so the cycle continues. The politics of difference leads each group to pick at the vulnerabilities of the other.

Men and women who run universities—whites, mostly—participate in the politics of difference because they handle their guilt differently than do many of their students. They don't deny it, but still they don't want to *feel* it. And to avoid this feeling of guilt they have tended to go along with whatever blacks put on the table rather than work with them to assess their real needs. University administrators have too often been afraid of guilt and have relied on negotiation and capitulation more to appease their own guilt than to help blacks and other minorities. Administrators would never give white students a racial theme dorm where they could be "more comfortable with people of their own kind," yet more and more universities are doing this for black students, thus fostering a kind of voluntary segregation. To avoid the anxieties of integrated situations blacks ask for theme dorms; to avoid guilt, white administrators give theme dorms.

When everyone is on the run from their anxieties about race, race relations on campus can be reduced to the negotiation of avoidances. A pattern of demand and concession develops in which both sides use the other to escape themselves. Black studies departments, black deans of student affairs, black counseling programs, Afro houses, black theme dorms, black homecoming dances and graduation ceremonies—black students and white administrators have slowly engineered a machinery of separatism that, in the name of sacred difference, redraws the ugly lines of segregation.

Black students have not sufficiently helped themselves, and universities, despite all their concessions, have not really done much for blacks. If both faced their anxieties, I think they would see the same thing: academic parity with all other groups should be the overriding mission of black students, and it should also be the first goal that universities have for their black students. Blacks can only *know* they are as good as others when they are, in fact, as good—when their grades are higher and their dropout rate lower. Nothing under the sun will substitute for this, and no amount of concessions will bring it about.

Universities can never be free of guilt until they truly help black students, which means leading and challenging them rather than negotiating and capitulating. It means inspiring them to achieve academic parity, nothing less, and helping them to see their own weaknesses as their greatest challenge. It also means dismantling the machinery of separatism, breaking the link between difference and power, and skewing the formula for entitlement away from race and gender and back to constitutional rights.

As for the young white students who have rediscovered swastikas and the word "nigger," I think that they suffer from an exaggerated sense of their own innocence, as if they were incapable of evil and beyond the reach of guilt. But it is also true that the politics of difference creates an environment that threatens their innocence and makes them defensive. White students are not invited to the negotiating table from which they see blacks and others walk away with concessions. The presumption is that they do not deserve to be there because they are white. So they can only be defensive, and the less mature among them will be aggressive. Guerrilla activity will ensue. Of course this is wrong, but it is also a reflection of an environment where difference carries power and where whites have the wrong "difference."

I think universities should emphasize commonality as a higher value than "diversity" and "pluralism"—buzzwords for the politics of difference. Difference that does not rest on a clearly delineated foundation of commonality is not only inaccessible to those who are not part of the ethnic or racial group, but also antagonistic to them. Difference can enrich only the common ground.

Integration has become an abstract term today, having to do with little more than numbers and racial balances. But it once stood for a high and admirable set of values. It made difference second to commonality, and it asked members of all races to face whatever fears they inspired in each other. I doubt the word will have a new vogue, but the values, under whatever name, are worth working for.

9

The Memory of Enemies

---◼---

"One of the most time-consuming things
is to have an enemy."

—E. B. WHITE

It is only human to give our enemies a distinct territory in
our memory, which is why we hear the buzz of summer's first
mosquito with mild alarm. We think only fools don't remember
their enemies, because remembering is preparedness. And,
conversely, what we call preparedness is often really a readi-
ness to remember the enemy, an openness to his memory-
triggering buzz. Even today, changing planes in a Southern
airport, the sound of a white Southern accent slips right past
what I know about the New South and finds my memory of
the old South. Recently, in line to buy a newspaper at such
an airport, I found myself carefully watching the white saleswoman, whose accent was particularly thick. If she was anything less than gracious to me as the lone black in line, I
knew my defenses would come alive. I would think she must
be of the Old South at heart, no more than a carpetbagger in
the new one. And how many others down here were like her,

imposters in this public relations bromide of a New South? If she put my change on the counter rather than in my hand, I'd have all the evidence I needed to close the case against her and the New South to boot.

I could condemn this woman, or at least be willing to condemn her and even her region, not because of her racial beliefs, which I didn't know, but because her accent had suddenly made her accountable to *my* voluminous and vivid memory of a racist South. Because of this accent and my Northern lack of familiarity with it, I was not encountering the woman so much as my own memory of an extremely powerful and dreaded enemy—the Old South. A flood of emotional images accompanied the memory, constituted it, and I saw right through the woman as if into a screen of memory. Coolly, I circled her with mistrust, ready for what I remembered. I thought I might take the offensive and let her glimpse the slightest disdain in the cut of my eyes. But, at the sight of this mistrustful black man, his eyes verging on disdain, might she not fall under the spell of her own enemy-memory and see before her an arrogant, hostile black against whom she must put up her own chilliness as a defense?

I think one of the heaviest weights that oppression leaves on the shoulders of its former victims is simply the memory of itself. This memory is a weight because it pulls the oppression forward, out of history and into the present, so that the former victim may see his world as much through the memory of his oppression as through his experience in the present. What makes this a weight is that the rememberer will gird himself against a larger and more formidable enemy than the one he is actually encountering. It was the intrusion of the enemy-memory that led me into an exaggerated and wasteful defensiveness with the saleswoman. I was willing to manufacture a little drama of one-upmanship, play it out, and then no doubt brood over it as though something was really at stake. Later, I might recount it to my friends and thereby give this battle with memory even more solidity. The enemy-memory clamors to be made real, demands that we work at its realization. And in this working is its real heaviness, since scarce resources are lost in unnecessary defense. Fortunately, in this situation, I caught myself and did not show this woman any disdain. She sold me the newspaper, put three quarters change into my hand, and gave me the same abbreviated, management-encouraged smile she had given everyone else before me. These little battles with memory can also be deflating.

I believe that one of the greatest problems black Americans currently face—one of the greatest barriers to our development in society—is that our memory of oppression has such power, magnitude, depth, and nuance that it constantly drains our best resources into more defense than is strictly necessary. Between defense and development, guns and butter, the enemy-memory perpetuates a costly imbalance in the distribution of energies, thoughts, and actions. None of this is to say that the real enemy has entirely disappeared. Nor is it to suggest that we should forget our oppression, assuming this was even possible. It is only to say that our oppression has left us with a dangerously powerful memory of itself that can pull us into warlike defensiveness at a time when there is more opportunity for development than ever before.

The memory of any enemy is always a pull into the past, into a preparedness against what has already happened. Some of this is necessary. But when there is a vast lake of such memory—and I can think of no group with a more powerful collective memory of its enemy than black Americans—the irresistible pull into the past can render opportunities in the present all but invisible. The look is backward rather than forward, outward rather than inward, so that the possibilities for development—education, economic initiative, job training, et cetera—are only seen out of the corner of the backward-looking eye. Thus, between 1976 and 1989, blacks have endured a drop in college enrollment of between 53 and 36 percent while white enrollment increased 3.6 percent. I don't suggest that the backward pull of memory fully accounts for a statistic this dramatic. But neither does it make sense to blame so profound a drop entirely on the shift in financial aid from grants to loans that occurred in the 1980s. White enrollment increased slightly under this same shift.

There are clearly many factors at work in a statistic like this. One of them, I believe, is a certain unseeing casualness toward opportunity that in itself has many sources, one being a powerful collective memory that can skew the vision of blacks away from the self-interested exploitation of opportunity and into a reenactment of past victimization that confirms our exaggerated sense of the enemy but also undermines our advancement. Not only does the enemy-memory pull us backward, it also indirectly encourages us to remain victims so as to confirm the power of the enemy we remember and believe in. It asks that we duplicate our oppression so that our remembered sense of it might be validated. I think this has something to do with the fact that so many middle-income black students decline to be admitted to colleges that woo them with preferential admissions policies. And for black students who are admitted, the national dropout rate is near 70 percent. If this is nothing less than a flight from opportunity, it is also a flight into a remembered victimization, a position we are used to and one that makes memory into reality.

I think the literary term "objective correlative" best describes the process by which our memory of the enemy pulls the past forward into the present. The white Southern accent I heard in the airport is an example of an objective correlative—an objective event that by association evokes a particular emotion or set of emotions. It was the savvy, musical sound of this woman's accent—an utterly objective and random event—that evoked in me an aggregate of troublesome racial emotions. The accent was a correlative to those emotions by virtue of association alone.

The black comedian Richard Pryor does a funny bit on this. To get away from the pressures and the racism he found on the mainland, he bought a house deep in the forest on a remote Hawaiian island. But just as he settles in one night to at last enjoy his solitude, he hears from the surrounding forest the infamous cry of the Southern "redneck"—"YAAA-HOO!" This was the chilling cry that often preceded an escapade of mindless violence against blacks, the sort of good ole boy violence that could mean anything from harassment to lynching. It correlates with and evokes the sort of terror that blacks lived with for centuries in the South, a terror that Pryor milks for great comic effect. But, as far as we know, there are no real good ole boys in his forest. The shout is by someone who does not know the meaning it carries for Pryor. It is an objective event that by correlation pulls forward a historical terror through space and time.

The enemy-memory works by correlation, by connecting events in the present to emotionally powerful memories of the enemy. In American life there are objective correlatives everywhere that evoke the painful thicket of emotions—vulnerability, self-doubt, helplessness, terror, and rage—that comes from having lived for centuries under the dominion of an enemy race. In the American language itself there are countless words and expressions that function as correlatives—"you people," "bootstraps," "reverse discrimination," "colored people" (interestingly "people of color" is not a correlative), "black militant," "credit to his race," "one of my best friends . . . ," "I never knew a black until college . . . the Army . . ."—any phrase or tone that condescends, damns with faint praise, or stereotypes either positively or negatively. Any generalization about blacks correlates with the practice of generalizing about us that led to our oppression. And then there is an entire iconography of visual correlatives covering everything from Confederate flags and pickup trucks with gun racks to black lawn jockeys, flesh-colored Band-Aids that are actually pink, separate black and white advertisements for the same product, et cetera. Tragically, the most relentless visual correlative may be white skin itself, especially for blacks with little experience in the larger society.

Blacks grow up in America surrounded by correlatives to their collective pain. I think the recent demand on college campuses and in the workplace for more racial sensitivity is, among other things, a demand that whites become more sensitive to the myriad correlatives that put blacks in touch with painful emotions. White insensitivity in this area is a form of power, an unearned and unfair power that feels to blacks like another manifestation of their victimization. And in a sense it is, since white insensitivity in whatever form (and sometimes nothing can be more insensitive than a pained sensitivity that calls attention to itself) carries the power to diminish blacks, even when unintended. On one level the push for racial sensitivity is an attempt to offset the power whites have by birthright to compromise blacks with racial anxiety by ignoring the correlatives to that anxiety.

But objective correlatives are only one part of the process of correlation by which the enemy-memory operates. They are intrusive visitations through which the objective world causes us to feel our emotional history in a way that makes us insecure in the present, and so robs us of power. I believe this process also works in reverse, in a way that tries to restore power. That is, the enemy-memory becomes a force in its own right and actually creates correlatives for itself in the world—correlatives that reinforce its often exaggerated sense of the enemy's power so as to justify black demands for power. In this process, mistrust is the transforming agent that encircles an "event" and redefines it as a correlative to the enemy's continuing intention to oppress blacks. And when the memory of the enemy is as vast and powerful as it is for black Americans, there is an abundance of mistrust available for this purpose. Correlatives created by racial mistrust are subjective rather than objective, since they do not come from the objective world but rather are imposed on it. They are fabrications of racial mistrust in which current events are infused with the memory of a more powerful racism than exists today.

A recent and striking example of this is the claim by many blacks that the drug epidemic in black neighborhoods across the country is the result of a white conspiracy to commit genocide against black people. Here the memory of pernicious racism is being brought forward to redefine a current problem, to transform it into a correlative for what is remembered so that it cannot be seen for what it is. Even if we assume that government is not doing all it can to combat drug use in the inner city, it takes a long stretch of the imagination to conclude that this is evidence of a white conspiracy to kill off blacks. I think memory and the mistrust born of it are the sources of this hyperbole. Also, once the black drug epidemic becomes a subjective correlative for black oppression, then it stands as a *racial* injustice and so entitles blacks, in the name of redress, to pursue power in relation to whites. Because subjective correlatives always make events into racial issues—by recasting them as examples of black victimization—they are always used to justify the pursuit of power.

All of this, I believe, has something to do with why the civil rights leadership has lost credibility in American society since the days of Martin Luther King. Too much under the sway of their memory of the enemy, this more recent group of leaders has not always made the distinction between hyperbolic correlatives for black oppression and actual oppressive events. When the NAACP marched against the recent group of Supreme Court decisions that severely limited preferential treatment programs, they transformed this cluster of decisions into a correlative for black oppression, even though at least one of them reaffirmed for whites the same constitutional right to sue for representation that blacks demanded during the civil rights movement. None of these decisions deprived blacks of their constitutional rights, so to characterize them as anti-black is to recast them, through memory and mistrust, into symbols of the kind of oppression that blacks knew in the days of *Plessey* v. *Ferguson*, when the principle of "separate but equal" was established. Decisions that attack *preferences* are made to correlate with decisions that deny black rights. Of course, this correlation is only suggested through the symbolism of protest marches and a rhetoric of black victimization, but its effect is to diminish the credibility of black leadership. Most Americans simply do not accept the correlation. It is an exaggeration that has the look of a power move.

The exaggeration of black victimization is always the first indication that a current event is being transformed by mistrust into a subjective correlative that sanctions the pursuit of racial power. (As discussed in the first chapter of this book, victimization is a form of innocence and innocence always entitles us to pursue power.) The current black leadership has injured its credibility by its tendency to make so many black problems into correlatives for black oppression. The epidemic of black teen pregnancies, the weakened black family, the decline in the number of black college students, and so on are too often cast as correlatives of historic racism. About Mayor Marion Barry's arrest on drug charges, Benjamin Hooks of the NAACP said, "I don't think there's any question there's some racism involved . . ." despite the fact that countless other black mayors have not been hounded by such charges. Such claims are exaggerations because racism simply does not fully explain these problems. No doubt they have something to do with the historic wounds of oppression, but what the charge of racism does not explain is the giving in to these wounds more than ever before during a twenty-five-year decline in racism and discrimination. There are more black males of college age in prison than in college, even as universities across the country struggle to recruit more black students. Black leaders can solve their "credibility gap" only by distinguishing between real oppression and those correlatives that exaggerate it in the interest of narrow racial power. Without this distinction our leaders seem always to be crying wolf. And here the point must be made that discrimination continues to exist, and we need a credible leadership to resist it.

Tragically, there is a real anti-black sentiment in American life, but it is no longer as powerful as we *remember* it to be. Our memory makes us like the man who wears a heavy winter coat in springtime because he was frostbitten in winter. Every sharp spring breeze becomes a correlative for the enemy of frostbite so that he is still actually living in winter even as flowers bloom all around him. Not only do subjective correlatives cause us to reenact the past, they also rarely bring us the power we seek through them because they are too much based on exaggeration. Worse, they cut us off from the present and its many opportunities by encouraging the sort of vision in which we look at the present only to confirm the past.

But the distortions of correlation are not the only problems that come to blacks from our enemy-memory. I think this memory has also led to one of our most serious mistakes in thinking: to often confuse the actual development of our race with the elimination of racial discrimination, to see somehow these two very different goals as synonymous. Though the elimination of discrimination clearly facilitates our development, the two goals are entirely different and require entirely different strategies. The elimination of discrimination will always be largely a collective endeavor, while racial development will always be the *effect* that results from individuals within the race bettering their own lives. The former requires group solidarity, collective action, and a positive group identity, while the latter demands individual initiative, challenging personal aspirations, focused hard work, and a strong individual identity. Different goals; different strategies. But I believe the powerful memories blacks have of racism and discrimination rally us to the fight against these things at the expense of our development as a people. This is one of the reasons why blacks have fallen further behind whites on many socioeconomic measures in the last twenty years, even as actual discrimination has declined.

The enemy-memory distracts us from development by miring us in a very natural process of *inversion* in which we invert from negative to positive the very point of difference—our blackness—that the enemy used to justify our oppression. Inversion tries to transform the quality that made us most vulnerable into an identity of invulnerability. Blackness becomes a source of pride rather than shame, strength rather than weakness. This is a necessary and inevitable process by which any oppressed group regathers dignity and esteem from the experience of denigration.

But inversion—fueled by the visceral memory of the enemy—is also a trap. (I must add that it is also fueled by the racial vulnerability discussed in chapters four and five. However, here I will focus on its connection to the enemy-memory.) The great evil of America's oppression of blacks was the use of the collective quality of color to limit us as individuals, no matter our talents or energies—individual autonomy stifled by oppressive collectivism. When inversion drives us to make our racial collectivity positive rather than negative, it may reach for new dignity, but it also reinforces our bondage to collectivism at the expense of individual autonomy. Whether we are struggling against shame or for pride, we are still spilling scarce energy into the pursuit of collective esteem at the expense of individual development.

Inversion draws us back into a preoccupation with our

collective identity at the very moment when we most stand to gain from the initiative of individuals who are unburdened by too much collective obligation. To carry off inversion we must become self-conscious about the meaning of our race, we must redefine that meaning, invest it with an ideology and a politics, claim an essence for it, and look to it, as much as to ourselves, as a means to betterment. And, of course, this degree of racial preoccupation prepares the ground for intense factionalism within the race. Who has the best twist on blackness, the Black Muslims or the civil rights establishment, the cultural nationalists or the black Baptists, Malcolm X or Martin Luther King? And who is the most black, who the least? Within each faction is a racial orthodoxy that must be endlessly debated and defended, which rallies the faction against other factions while imposing a censorship of thought on its own members. Even when blacks avoid factions, they must be ready to defend that choice to others and to themselves. Inversion perpetuates the fundamental imbalance of racial oppression itself by giving the collective quality of race far too much importance in the lives of individual black Americans.

One of the many advantages whites enjoy in America is a relative freedom from the draining obligation of racial inversion. Whites do not have to spend precious time fashioning an identity out of simply being white. They do not have to self-consciously imbue whiteness with an ideology, look to whiteness for some special essence, or divide up into factions and wrestle over what it means to be white. Their racial collectivism, to the extent that they feel it, creates no imbalance between the collective and the individual. This, of course, is yet another blessing of history and of power, of never having lived in the midst of an overwhelming enemy race. It is a blessing won at the expense of blacks, whose subjugation brought whites a sort of automatic racial inversion—a secure sense of superiority that freed them from the struggle for simple racial dignity.

It was clearly impossible for blacks to avoid inversion, just as it was impossible for us to avoid our enemy. Therefore it was also impossible for us to avoid the burden of collectivism and the preoccupation with race that goes with it. Inversion once was a survival impulse, and yet, today, when the oppression of blacks has greatly diminished, I believe this impulse causes our most serious strategic mistake: to put the responsibility for our racial development more in the hands of the collective than in the hands of the individuals who compose it. It is inversion that obscures the distinction mentioned above between the elimination of discrimination (societal change) and racial development by submerging us too deeply in collectivism. And once "collectivized," collective action seems to be the only remedy for our problems. But, while civil rights bills can be won this way, only the individual can achieve in school, master a salable skill, open a business, become an accountant or an engineer. Despite our collective oppression, opportunities for development can finally be exploited only by individuals.

Whether a stigmatized minority group develops successfully or slips into inertia has much to do with whether or not the group allows its impulse toward inversion (and therefore collectivism) to muddy the distinction between societal change and group development. This is the distinction that allows the group to assign responsibility for development to the individual. Those groups that have somehow maintained this distinction (for historical and cultural reasons too complex to explore here) have thrived in America despite racism, anti-

Semitism, and outright discrimination. Asians, Jews, West Indians, and others have found their avenue for development in the aspirations of their individuals who have approached American society with initiative, energy, and pragmatism. Certainly, the point must be made here that the civil rights movement, which won many victories against discrimination, made the road easier for the individuals within these groups. On the front of collective action against bigotry, no group has made a greater contribution than black Americans. Yet I think the extremely intense memory of our enemy (along with racial vulnerability and the continuing presence of racism in America) has so absorbed us into inversion and collectivism that we have overlooked the developmental power to be found in the aspirations of our individuals.

This imbalance is evident today in many areas of black life. Black college students often take a leading role in demanding change on their campuses, yet as a group they have the lowest grade point average and the highest dropout rate of any student group in America—collective action over individual initiative. The national civil rights leadership relentlessly pressures the government for more and better social programs, yet does not put equal pressure on blacks to achieve as individuals—one result being that we are often not developed enough to take advantage of the concessions civil rights leadership has won, such as affirmative action. Their unconscious strategy is to transform the problems of black America into subjective correlatives. When problems, like black teenage pregnancies, the drug epidemic, poor educational performance, and so on are recast as correlatives for black oppression, the primary responsibility for solving them automatically falls on the larger society. Subjective correlatives serve inversion by blame-placing, by casting blacks as victims and the society as their oppressor. But most of all they reinforce the collectivism of inversion by always showing black problems as resulting from an oppression that can only be resisted by collective action. And here is where the distinction between societal change and racial development is lost, where the individual is subsumed by the collective.

Thus, at the 1989 NAACP convention, the several problems that face black America—from affirmative action to teen pregnancies—were listed on the agenda, but primarily as subjective correlatives, as evidence of society's indifference to blacks, as yet more proof of our continuing victimization and, therefore, our innocence. In this deterministic context the power to be found in the individual is lost amid the exhortations for more societal change. The price blacks pay for inversion, for placing too much of the blame for our problems on society, is helplessness before those problems.

Inversion also hurts our development in another way. If the memory of the enemy leads to inversion (helped along by subjective correlatives), it is also true that inversion requires us to remember the enemy. In order to invert, to make blackness positive, we must know the negative views whites have of us. In this sense, inversion not only makes the black identity itself too much a response to white racism, but it also makes our identity dependent on that racism. With inversion we need a knowledge of our former oppressor's worst view of us in order to carry out the work of self-definition— a process that requires us to remember the enemy at his "worst" in order to know ourselves at our "best." In this way, inversion, born of the memory of our enemy, also demands that we remember him more, thus completing a self-perpetuating cycle of obsessive and painful memory.

By exaggerating our enemy in order to define ourselves,

we put ourselves in the ironic position of having to deny clearly visible opportunities in order to "be black" and claim a strong black identity. Out of this cycle of memory comes the "real black" who sees society as an oppressive withholder of black opportunities. I recently spoke with a black woman who described herself as a cultural nationalist. In her view there were virtually no opportunities for blacks to enter the mainstream of American life, which she saw as fundamentally racist. She was, as we say, the blackest of the black, yet this purified identity was achieved by an absolute denial of mainstream black opportunity. In her scheme, the more opportunity one admitted to, let alone took advantage of, the less "black" one was. The power of memory and inversion had virtually called this woman back to slavery and left her no option but collective action, since individual possibility was all but invisible to her. She was an extreme case, but also an extreme version of the paradigm that touches many blacks. Even among middle-class blacks who function well in the mainstream, when the time comes to declare one's identity, to announce one's blackness, there is invariably a denial of black opportunity. This is the denial that brings one securely back inside the circle of blackness, that quite literally lets one feel black. To point to opportunity is to stand outside this circle, to be less black. Inversion is a reunion with the enemy in which we once again define ourselves as his victim.

Common wisdom sometimes tells us that it is good to have enemies—"We can learn even from our enemies," said Ovid. Probably, this is true, since two other things are certainly true: we will have enemies whether they are good for us or not, and we will have a bond with them whether we wish to or not. But the quarrel I have with such wisdom is that it does not speak to the issue of degree. It is one thing simply to have an enemy; it is another thing to be inundated and sat upon by an enemy and to live in this condition over the course of centuries. The magnitude of such an enemy makes the common wisdom almost fatuous. No doubt, black Americans have learned much from such an enemy, but at a price that has been absurdly punitive. Still, I think we have one thing left to learn—to discipline our memory of the enemy so that we can distinguish between that memory and the actual "enemy activity" that we may still encounter. To fail in this distinction is to remain at war with a far greater enemy than the one we actually live with.

Our greatest problem today is insufficient development—this *more* than white racism. And just as nations deplete themselves rather than develop in wartime, we can't really advance under the burden of an enemy swollen into a Goliath by memory. I think we should see the enemy for the mad bee that he is rather than the raging lion he used to be. If this metaphor is too charitable, then we can pick another one, but in any case we must diminish his size and scope in our minds to his actual proportions. Then we must free our individuals from the tyranny of a wartime collectivism in which they must think of themselves as victims in order to identify with their race. The challenge now is to reclaim ourselves from the exaggerations of our own memory and to go forward as the free American citizens that we are. There is no magic that will make development happen. We simply have to want more for ourselves, be willing to work for it, and not use our enemy—old or new—as an excuse not to pursue it. It doesn't really matter that Southern accents in Southern airports make me remember. What's important is that I can travel.

Epilogue

I have mentioned in several places in this book that I was caught up in the new spirit of black power and pride that swept over black America in the late sixties like one of those storms that changes the landscape. I will always believe this storm was inevitable and, therefore, positive in many ways. What I gained from it was the power to be racially unapologetic, no mean benefit considering the long trial of patience that the civil rights movement subjected blacks to. But after awhile, by the early seventies, it became clear that black power did not offer much of a blueprint on how to move my life forward. Despite the strong feeling that it had given me a crucial part of myself, it told me virtually nothing about who I was as an individual or how I might live in the world as myself. Of course, it was my mistake to think it could. But in the late sixties, "blackness" was an invasive form of collective identity that cut so deeply into one's individual space that it seemed also to be an individual identity. It came as something of a disappointment to realize that the two could not be the same, that being "black" in no way spared me the necessity of being myself.

In the early seventies, without realizing it, I made a sort of bargain with the prevailing black identity—I subscribed in a general way to its point of view so that I could be free to get on with my life. Many other blacks I knew made this same bargain, got on with their lives and fellow-traveled with black power. I don't believe this subscription was insincere, but it was convenient since it opened the individual space out of which we could make our lives.

And what were we subscribing to? Generally, I think it was a form of black identity grounded in the spirit of black power. It carried a righteous anger at and mistrust of American society. It believed that blacks continued to be the victims of institutional racism, that we would have to maintain an adversarial stance toward society, and that a tight racial unity was necessary both for survival and advancement. This identity was, and is, predicated on the notion that those who burned you once will burn you again, and it presupposes a deep racist reflex in American life that will forever try to limit black possibility.

I think it was the space I cleared for myself by loosely subscribing to this identity that ultimately put me in conflict with it. It is in the day-to-day struggle of living on the floor of a society, so to speak, that one gains a measure of what is possible in that society. And by simply living as an individual in America—with my racial identity struggle suspended by my subscription to the black power identity—I discovered that American society offered me and blacks in general a remarkable range of opportunity if we were willing to pursue it.

In my daily life I continue to experience racial indignities and slights. This morning I was told that blacks had too much musical feeling (soul, I suppose) to be good classical musicians; yesterday I passed two houses with gnomish little black lawn jockeys on the front porch; my children have been called "nigger," not to mention myself; I wear a tie and carry a professorial briefcase so my students on the first day of class will know I'm the teacher; and so on. I also know that actual racial discrimination persists in many areas of American life. I have been the victor in one housing-discrimination suit, as were my parents before me. And, certainly, garden variety racism is still a tonic for the inadequate white. In my daily life I have no immunity from any of this. What is more, I do not like it, nor will I ever endure it with élan. Yet I have also come to realize that in this same society, I have been more in charge of my fate than I always wanted to believe, and that though I have been limited by many things, my race was not foremost among them.

The point is that both realities are true. There is still racial insensitivity and some racial discrimination against blacks in this society, but there is also much opportunity. What brought me into conflict with the prevailing black identity was that it was almost entirely preoccupied with the former to the exclusion of the latter. The black identity I was subscribing to in the seventies—and that still prevails today—was essentially a "wartime" identity shaped in the confrontational sixties. It presumed that black opportunity was sharply limited by racism and that blacks had to "win" more "victories" "against" society before real opportunity would open up. This was an identity that still saw blacks as victims and that kept them at war with society even as new possibilities for advancement opened all around. Worse, by focusing so exclusively on white racism and black victimization, it implied that our fate was in society's control rather than our own, and that opportunity itself was something that was given rather than taken. This identity robs us of the very self-determination we have sought for so long, and deepens our dependency on the benevolence of others.

Why do we cling to an adversarial, victim-focused identity that preoccupies us with white racism? I think because of fear, self-doubt, and simple inexperience. As I've discussed elsewhere in this book, I believe we carry an inferiority anxiety that makes the seizing of opportunity more risky for us, since setbacks and failures may seem to confirm inferiority. To avoid this risk we may hold a victim-focused identity that tells us there is less opportunity than there really is. Our culture was formed in oppression rather than in freedom, which means we are somewhat inexperienced in the full use of freedom, in seeing possibilities and developing them. In oppression we were punished for having initiative and thereby conditioned away from it. Also, our victimization itself has been our primary source of power in society—the basis of our demands for redress—and the paradoxical result of relying on this source of power is that it rewards us for continuing to see ourselves as victims of a racist society. So our victim-focused identity serves us by preserving our main source of power and by shielding us from our fear of inferiority and our relative inexperience with the challenges of freedom.

And yet this leaves us with an identity that is at war with our own best interests, that magnifies our oppression and diminishes our sense of possibility. I think this identity is a weight on blacks because it is built around our collective insecurity rather than our faith in our human capacity to seize opportunity as individuals. It amounts to a self-protective collectivism that obsesses us with black unity instead of individual initiative. To be "black" in this identity, one need only manifest the symbols, postures, and rhetoric of black unity. Not only is personal initiative unnecessary for being "black," but the successful exercise of initiative—working one's way into the middle class, becoming well-off, gaining an important position—may in fact jeopardize one's "blackness," make one somehow less black. The poor black is the true black; the successful black is more marginally black unless he (or she) frequently announces his solidarity with the race in the way politicians declare their patriotism. This sort of identity never works, never translates into the actual uplift of black people. It confuses racial unity with initiative by relying on unity to do what only individual initiative can do. Uplift can only come when many millions of blacks seize the possibilities inside the sphere of their personal lives and use them to take themselves forward. Collectively, we can resist oppression, but racial development will always be, as Ralph Ellison once put it, "the gift of its individuals."

The collective black identity fogs up the sacred line between the individual and the collective. To find my own individuality, I had to do what many blacks in fact do—push the collective out of my individual space by subscribing to an identity I wasn't living by. Many blacks maintain their "blackness" as a sort of union card while actually living by principles and values that are classically American and universal to the middle class everywhere: hard work, self-reliance, initiative, property ownership, family ties, and so on. In pushing the collective identity out of our individual space, we are also pushing back the diminished sense of possibility that it carries in order to take advantage of the broader field of possibility that our actual experience shows us is there.

To retrieve our individuality and find opportunity, blacks today must—consciously or unconsciously—disregard the prevailing victim-focused black identity. Though it espouses black pride, it is actually a repressive identity that generates a victimized self-image, curbs individualism and initiative, diminishes our sense of possibility, and contributes to our demoralization and inertia. It is a skin that needs shedding.

There are many profound problems facing black America today—a swelling black underclass, a black middle class that declined slightly in the eighties, a declining number of black college students, an epidemic of teenage pregnancy, drug use, and gang violence, continuing chronic unemployment, astoundingly high college and high school dropout rates, an increasing number of single-parent families, a disproportionately high infant mortality rate, and so on. Against all this it seems almost esoteric to talk about identity and possibility. Yet, in this book, I have tried to look at the underlying network of attitudes, pressures, and anxieties that have deepened our problems even as more opportunity has opened up to us. Without understanding these intangibles, I don't think we can easily know what to do.

Many remedies have been tried. Here and there various social programs, "interventions," have worked. Many more programs and policies have not worked. Clearly we should find the ones that do work and have more of them. But my deepest feeling is that, in a society of increasingly limited resources, there will never be enough programs to meet the need. What I really believe is that we black Americans will never be saved or even assisted terribly much by others, never be repaid for our suffering, and never find that symmetrical, historical justice that we cannot help but long for. These things will never happen. Jean-Paul Sartre once said that we were the true "existential people," and certainly we have always had to create ourselves out of whole cloth and find our own means for survival. Nothing has really changed.

I think the most cursory glance at the list of problems that blacks now face reveals that we are in a kind of despair. The evidence of this is everywhere, from the college campuses— where black students are five times more likely than whites to drop out—to the black underclass where a miasma of drug addiction, violence, and hopelessness has already transformed many inner cities into hearts of darkness. I have written in this book about some of the sources of this despair, but I also believe that they all pressure us into a single overriding mistake: a hesitation before the challenges of self-interested, individual action. It is at the point of taking self-interested action in the American mainstream that all the unresolved wounds of oppression manifest themselves and become a wall. Here is where inferiority anxiety, a victim-focused identity, that peculiar mix of personal and racial self-doubt, fear of failure, and even self-hate all combine to make for a fear of self-interested action. And without such action, there can only be despair and inertia.

There will be no end to despair and no lasting solution to any of our problems until we rely on individual effort within the American mainstream—rather than collective action against the mainstream—as our means of advancement. We need a collective identity that encourages diversity within the race, that does not make black unity a form of repression, that does not imply that the least among us are the most black, and that makes the highest challenge of "blackness" personal development. This identity must be grounded also in the reality that I and many other blacks have discovered in the space of our individual lives: that there is today, despite America's residual racism, an enormous range of opportunity open to blacks in this society. The nexus of this new identity must be a meeting of black individual initiative and American possibility.

I believe black leadership must make this nexus its primary focus. They must preach it, tell it, sell it, and demand it. Our leadership has looked at government and white society very critically. Now they must help us look at ourselves. We need our real problems named and explained; otherwise, we have no chance to overcome them. Their impulse is to be "political," to keep the larger society on edge, to keep them feeling as though they have not done enough for blacks. And, clearly, they have not. But the price they pay for this form of "politics" is to keep blacks focused on an illusion of deliverance by others, and no illusion weakens us more. Our leaders must take a risk. They must tell us the truth, tell us of the freedom and opportunity they have discovered in their own lives. They must tell us what they tell their own children when they go home at night: to study hard, pursue their dreams with discipline and effort, to be responsible for themselves, to have concern for others, to cherish their race and at the same time make their own lives as Americans. When our leaders put a spotlight on our victimization and seize upon our suffering to gain us ineffectual concessions, they inadvertently turn themselves into enemies of the truth, not to mention enemies of their own people.

I believe that black Americans are infinitely freer today than ever before. This is not a hope; this is a reality, an extremely hard-won reality. Many of our great leaders, and countless foot soldiers with them, died for this reality. Racial hatred has not yet left the American landscape. Who knows how or when this deliverance will occur? Yet the American black, supported by a massive body of law and the not inconsiderable goodwill of his fellow citizens, is basically as free as he or she wants to be. For every white I have met who is a racist, I have met twenty more who have seen me as an equal. And of those twenty, ten have only wished me the best as an individual. This I say, as opposed to confessing, has been my actual reality. I believe it is time for blacks to begin the shift from a wartime to a peacetime identity, from fighting for opportunity to the seizing of it. The immutable fact of late twentieth-century life is that it *is* there for blacks to seize. Martin Luther King did not live to experience this. But, of course, on the night before he died he seemed to know he would not. From the mountaintop he had looked-over and seen the promised land, but then he said, "I may not get there with you . . ." I won't say we are snuggled deep in the promised valley he saw beyond the mountain. Every day things remind me that we are not. But I also know that we have it over our greatest leader. We are on the other side of his mountaintop, on the downward slope toward the valley he saw. This is something we ought to know. But what we must know even more than this is that nothing on this earth can be promised but a chance. The promised land guarantees nothing. It is only an opportunity, not a deliverance.